The Life
of
Jesus Christ

THE LIFE
OF
JESUS CHRIST

A Continuous Account from the
Four Gospels and Acts

Arranged and Annotated by
Albert J. Nevins, M.M.

Text and Footnotes from
The Living Bible

Huntington, IN

COSTELLO PUBLISHING CO., INC.
P.O. Box 9
Northport, N.Y. 11768

The Living Bible, © 1971
Tyndale House Publishers, Wheaton, Illinois
Used by permission

ISBN: 0-87973-500-7

Cover design and illustration by Jeff R. Thurau, Roth Advertising, Inc.

Manufactured for Our Sunday Visitor by Costello Publishing Co., Inc.

Contents

1. THE BIRTH AND CHILDHOOD OF JESUS CHRIST

2. THE BEGINNING OF THE MISSION

3. ORGANIZING THE KINGDOM

Contents

Contents

Contents

Introduction

What This Book Is About

All that we know about Jesus Christ comes to us from the New Testament. The term "New Testament" was originated by Jesus Himself as recorded in both the King James and Douay translations of Lk 22:20. More recent translations render this term "New Covenant." Jesus used the term in contrast to the Old Covenant or Old Testament, made between God and Abraham and again with Moses.

There are four accounts of the life of Jesus in the New Testament, sometimes dealing with the same material, sometimes recounting it from different viewpoints, and sometimes using material exclusive to the one telling the story. There are differences in emphasis, in chronology, and in detail.

The purpose of this book is to give one unified continuous account of the life of Jesus, using the work of four different writers. The text used is that of *The Living Bible* and the author has added nothing of his own. It is hoped that this will make the story of Jesus more complete and understandable, and that it will lead the reader to examine the original accounts to discover the unique viewpoint each sacred writer brought to his task.

The Gospels

The word "gospel" is from the old Anglo-Saxon "godspell" which meant "good news." The word itself was a rendering of the Latin *evangelium*, in turn from the Greek *euangelion*, which meant "good news" but came to be used for the message of Jesus Christ and then the accounts of His life.

There are four gospels or accounts of the life of Jesus (Matthew,

Mark, Luke and John) with a small amount of additional material in the Book of Acts. The Gospels of Matthew, Mark, and Luke are called synoptic gospels because they parallel one another, using similar material but from different viewpoints. Many of the passages are almost exactly the same.

None of the evangelists set out to write a biography of Jesus as we understand that word today. They were primarily concerned with the good news—the teaching of Jesus Christ and His resurrection. They used events from His life to show His personality so that we might better understand His death and resurrection.

The Gospel of Mark

In recent years, scholars have generally come to the opinion that the Gospel of Mark was the first Gospel written and that it was used by Matthew and Luke in the composition of their works. It was composed about A.D. 65, although some scholars have even placed it earlier. The traditional place of authorship is Rome. The audience intended was non-Jews outside of Palestine.

The purpose of the work is to show that Jesus Christ is the Son of God. The Gospel is attributed to John Mark, the son of a certain Mary at whose home in Jerusalem the early Christians gathered. He was the cousin of Barnabas and he traveled with Barnabas and Paul on the latter's first missionary journey. He is said to have been a disciple of Peter from whom he drew material to form the Gospel. He may have been a witness to some of the events he describes.

The Gospel of Matthew

This Gospel appears first in the New Testament because it was believed to have been the first one written. Today it is ranked second and the date of its composition placed about the year A.D. 70. Its audience was the Jewish Christians of Palestine and Syria. Its purpose was to show that Jesus is the promised Messiah. The best guess as to its place of origin is Syria.

Early tradition assigned its authorship to the Apostle Matthew, also called Levi, a tax collector who after his conversion gave a banquet for Jesus. Some modern scholars hold that the author was a Jewish Christian other than Matthew who wrote from a tradition credited to Matthew. There is no hard evidence of this fact other than it was a common practice in New Testament times for an author to assign his work to some prominent person.

The Gospel of Luke

The date given for the Gospel of Luke is between A.D. 70–80. Like that of Mark, it was written for Gentile Christians. Its purpose was to develop and give more information than that found in Mark and Matthew.

Luke particularly gives us most of what we know of the prebirth of Jesus and his early years. He also went to great effort to give us the words of Jesus, particularly His parables. No one seriously challenges Luke as author of the Gospel bearing his name or of the Book of Acts. Paul calls him ''our most dear physician'' (Col 4:14). He was a fellow worker of Paul's, traveled with him, and was with him in Rome.

The Gospel of John

There is much internal evidence to show that the Gospel of John was written for a Jewish audience to prove that Jesus is not only the promised Messiah but also the Son of God. The date given for its composition is about A.D. 90. The author identifies himself as ''the disciple whom Jesus loved'' and as an eyewitness to many of the events he describes.

The tradition from the earliest days said that this disciple was John the Apostle. Some modern critics have argued for another author—a disciple of John or someone else named John—but conclusions are without proof. The Gospel of John is more theological than the Synoptics. John's father was Zebedee, a fisherman. John and his brother, James, became early disciples of Jesus. He is the only apostle who stayed with Jesus during His crucifixion.

Palestine in the Time of Jesus

The word "Palestine" derives from the Hebrew term for the Philistines. Although it originally only applied to the coastal area around Gaza, the Greeks and Romans enlarged the term to Syria Palestina, which embraced the area south of Damascus and corresponded to Canaan, the Promised Land of the Jews. This is an area of about nine thousand square miles, the size of New Hampshire. At the time Jesus lived there, the area held about one-half million to two million people, according to acceptable estimates.

When Jesus was born, the land was ruled by Herod the Great, whose kingdom included Judea, Samaria, Galilee, Perea, and some northern regions now part of Syria and Jordan. It was bounded by the Mediterranean Sea and Phoenicia on the west, desert to the east, Syria to the north, and Egypt to the south.

The area is divided into three parts, running north to south. There is the western coastal plain with its semi-tropical climate, much like southern Florida. Then comes a line of hills and mountains that extend from the mountains of Lebanon. This high country has damp, cold winters, and snow is not unusual. Third is the rich Jordan Valley with its pleasant winters but very hot summers.

Throughout history Palestine has had great importance because it was the land bridge between Europe and Africa. Caravans of trade came from the east, north, and south. Because of its strategic importance, conquerors—Assyrian, Babylonian, Persian, Greek, and Roman—sought to control it. The people of the area were well acquainted with foreign invaders.

The Political Situation

The Roman legions under Pompey took control of Palestine in 63 B.C.. Pompey was succeeded by Julius Caesar and he in turn by Octavian Augustus, who was the emperor when Jesus was born. Herod the Great was appointed king by the Romans in 40 B.C. and it was he who restored the Temple in Jerusalem. Herod died in 4 B.C. while Jesus was in Egypt, a refugee from Herod's wrath.

After the death of Herod the Great, the Romans divided the kingdom and appointed his sons to rule certain areas. Because Judea was the heart of the region, the Romans kept tight control there and eventually sent their own governor (procurator), Pontius Pilate, who was to condemn Jesus to death. During the ministry of Jesus, Herod Antipas was tetrarch of Galilee and Perea (4 B.C. to A.D. 39). He is the ruler who ordered the beheading of John the Baptist and before whom Christ was brought after His arrest. Tiberius was the Roman emperor at this time.

The Religious Situation in Jerusalem

From the time David had made Jerusalem his capital and brought the Ark there, the city was always the center for Jewish political and religious life. Built on a ridge, with natural defenses, it was closely connected to Jewish history. It was here that the priest-king, Melchizedek offered his unbloody sacrifice. To this area came Abraham and it is said that he prepared to sacrifice his son, Isaac, on the hill where the Temple was later built.

The Temple

If Jerusalem was the center for the national life of the Jewish people, the Temple was the heart of its religious life. The first great Temple had been built by King Solomon. It was destroyed by Babylonian invaders. When the people returned from exile, the Second Temple was built. It was to suffer profanations, abominations, and disrepair over the centuries. The Maccabees restored it, only to have it later sacked by Crassus and again by Lysimachus.

Although Herod the Great was at heart a pagan and in practice a cynic, he knew the depth of Jewish religious feeling. To win Jewish support and for his own vainglory, Herod built the Third Temple, the magnificent structure that Jesus knew. The Temple became a unifying force for the Jews.

It is estimated that in the time of Jesus there were seven thousand Temple priests, assisted by eleven thousand Levites. The main use of the Temple was to offer sacrifices of atonement. The daily sacrifices were accompanied by hymns of praise and worship, the reading of the Law and various prayers. The Temple was the goal of pilgrims from all parts of Palestine and beyond.

Religious Bodies

Religious government was exercised through the Sanhedrin, the supreme religious assembly or council. Originally a body of priests and aristocrats, it was in the time of Jesus an assembly of seventy members made up of priests, Pharisees, Sadducees, scribes, and elders (family or tribal heads), and it was presided over by a high priest. Under Herod and the Romans the authority of the Sanhedrin was restricted and capital crimes were removed from its jurisdiction.

Pharisees

The name, meaning ''separated,'' was probably given to the group because their strict and exact interpretation of the law set them apart from less legalistic Jews. The Pharisees accepted not only the written law but also the oral law (the traditions of the ancients). They believed in the resurrection, in angels and demons, and in human freedom under divine guidance. Their influence far exceeded their numbers, which the historian, Josephus, places at six thousand.

Sadducees

The Sadducees came from the priestly aristocracy. They longed for the return of priestly rule in Israel, which would make them rulers. They were political only to preserve priestly wealth and power. They disagreed with the Pharisees, denying oral tradition and admitting only the written law. They denied the resurrection of the body, angels and evil spirits, and divine Providence.

Scribes

The Scriptures had to be copied by hand and this was the task of the Scribes. They were also called upon to interpret the Scriptures, and their decisions became known as the oral laws. Because they worked so closely with the Scriptures, they were recognized as religious lawyers and were the type of lawyers whom Jesus encountered and condemned.

The Essenes

Since the discovery of the Dead Sea (Qumran) Scrolls we have learned a great deal about the Essenes, a religious sect that lived a community life near the Dead Sea. They were ascetics, legalistic and rigid. They believed they were the true interpreters of the law and the prophets. Because there is some resemblance between Qumran texts and some parts of the gospel, some believe that Jesus was acquainted with their teachings. Some also hold that John the Baptist may have been a member of this group.

The Zealots

The Zealots were revolutionists in the tradition of the Maccabees. They gave a religious cast to rebellion against Rome. Many of their members were arrested, and it was a Zealot, Menahem, who was the leader of the Jews' last stand at Masada against the Romans. Simon, the Apostle, was a Zealot.

Herodians

The Herodians were more political than religious. They backed the house of Herod and Roman rule in the hope that the Romans would restore authority over Palestine to the Herods.

The Synagogue

It is believed that the synagogue (Greek, *synagoge*, meeting place) began during the Jewish exile when the people needed a place to instruct their children in the law and for their own worship. After the exile synagogues were developed for towns where the people could not easily get to the Temple, for Jewish communities living outside Palestine, and even for the people of Jerusalem itself, as adjuncts to the Temple.

Synagogues were not governed by priests but by a committee of elders. Services were conducted by the people themselves. In each synagogue was an ark or chest where the sacred scrolls of the law were kept. Meetings were held on the Sabbath and feast days. The service began with the *shema*, a type of Jewish creed. A passage from the Torah scrolls was read, followed by a sermon or discourse of explanation. The entire law was covered in a three-year period. Jesus frequently used the synagogue for His own preaching.

Calendar and Festivals

The Jewish year followed a solar-lunar calendar. The days began at sunset and months began on each new moon. The year went from one equinox to the next. In ancient time the first month (Nisan) corresponded roughly to our March 15–April 15.

The most important day of the week was the Sabbath (our Saturday). It is not known when the Sabbath arose but it existed in the time of the Book of Exodus. It was a day when work ceased. The piety of the Jew could be judged by the strictness of the Sabbath observance. It was the seventh day of the week for Jews, and this was a reminder of the seventh day on which God rested from the work of creation. On this weekly feast the people assembled for worship and instruction in the Temple and in their synagogues. In addition, there were special feasts throughout the year.

Feast of Passover

The Feast of Passover began, in ancient times, on the fourteenth day of the first month. (Passover begins in the seventh month, according to the contemporary Jewish calendar.) Although its roots go back to pre-Exodus times, in the days of Jesus it was a pilgrimage feast commemorating the deliverance of Israel from Egypt. Outside of the synagogue it was celebrated with a family dinner (*seder*), reliving that terrible night in Egypt when God passed over the Jewish homes and spared them.

Feast of Unleavened Bread

On the next day after Passover, the Feast of Unleavened Bread began. It originated as a harvest feast of thanksgiving. For the next seven days, bread had to be made without leaven. The feast was celebrated by offering a sheaf of newly cut grain to God. With Passover, it made an eight-day commemoration.

Feast of Weeks (Pentecost)

After seven full weeks passed from the Feast of Unleavened Bread, the fiftieth day was celebrated as the Feast of Weeks. It was a harvest thanksgiving festival. It was a day of rejoicing on which sacrifices of animals, leavened bread and grain were offered. It also commemorated God's covenant with Israel.

Feast of Tabernacles (Tents or Booths)

This feast came at the end of the harvest and was another feast of thanksgiving to God. The autumn festival lasted for seven days. Although Exodus had generally fixed it as the time when the harvest was finished, its beginning was later fixed to the fifteenth day of Tishri (September 15–October 15). Tents were built to remind Israel of its nomadic life in the wilderness.

Day of Atonement (Yom Kippur)

The most solemn day of the year was on the tenth day of Tishri (the seventh month). It was a day of fasting and penance, the only day of the year the High Priest entered the Holy of Holies in the Temple. Sacrifices of expiation were offered. The rite is described in Lev 16:1–34.

Feast of Purim

It was a two-day festival held on the fourteenth–fifteenth of Adar (February 15–March 15). It had a carnival atmosphere and commemorated the triumph of the Persian Jews over their persecutors (Est 9:17–22). It was not strictly a religious holiday.

Feast of Dedication (Hanukkah)

This was a relatively new feast, created by Judas Maccabeus to commemorate the rededication of the Temple, which had been profaned by Antiochus Epiphanes three years earlier. It was also called the Feast of Lights because people put lamps in front of their homes, adding one to each of the eight days of the feast. It took place on the twenty-fifth of Kislev (November 15–December 15).

Money

Because of the political situation in the time of Jesus there was a confusing number of money systems. Also because there was a large number of Jews living outside Palestine, when they returned home, they brought various coinage with them. As a result, money changers did a thriving business in Jerusalem.

The approximate value of money mentioned in the New Testament:

Mite: ¼ cent
Farthing: 1 cent
Denarius: 25 cents
Drachma: 25 cents
Shekel: 1 dollar
Talent: 1,500 dollars
A day's wage: 25 cents

Other Measurements

Finger: ¾ inch
Handbreadth: 3 inches
Span: 8.7 inches
Common cubit: 17.5 inches
Fathom: 6 feet
Furlong: 606 feet
Roman mile: 1,618 yards
A day's journey: 20 miles
A Sabbath Day's journey: 0.6 miles

THE LIFE
OF
JESUS CHRIST

A Continuous Account from the
Four Gospels and Acts

1.

THE BIRTH AND CHILDHOOD
OF JESUS CHRIST

Theological Introduction
Jn 1:1–18

[1]Before anything else existed,[a] there was Christ,[b] with God. [2]He has always[a] been alive and is himself God. [3]He created everything there is—nothing exists that he didn't make. [4]Eternal life is in him, and this life gives light to all mankind. [5]His life is the light that shines through the darkness—and the darkness can never extinguish it.

[6,7]God sent John the Baptist as a witness to the fact that Jesus Christ is the true Light. [8]John himself was not the Light; he was only a witness to identify it. [9]Later on, the one who is the true Light arrived to shine on everyone coming into the world.

[10]But although he made the world, the world didn't recognize him when he came. [11,12]Even in his own land and among his own people, the Jews, he was not accepted. Only a few would welcome and receive him. But to all who received him, he gave the right to become children of God. All they needed to do was to trust him to save them.[c] [13]All those who believe this are reborn!—not a physical rebirth[d] resulting from human passion or plan—but from the will of God.

[14]And Christ[b] became a human being and lived

Literally, "In the beginning was the Word." This is a theological statement by John. In the Old Testament God's revelation was in creation. In the New Testament it is Jesus Himself.

---

a. Literally, "In the beginning." b. Literally, "the Word," meaning Christ, the wisdom and power of God and the first cause of all things; God's personal expression of himself to men. c. Literally, "to believe on his name." d. Literally, "not of blood."

here on earth among us and was full of loving forgiveness[e] and truth. And some of us have seen his glory[f]—the glory of the only Son of the heavenly Father![g]

[15]John pointed him out to the people, telling the crowds, "This is the one I was talking about when I said, 'Someone is coming who is greater by far than I am—for he existed long before I did!'" [16]We have all benefited from the rich blessings he brought to us—blessing upon blessing heaped upon us! [17]For Moses gave us only the Law with its rigid demands and merciless justice, while Jesus Christ brought us loving forgiveness as well. [18]No one has ever actually seen God, but, of course, his only Son has, for he is the companion of the Father and has told us all about him.

An Angel Announces the Birth of Jesus' Cousin, John
Lk 1:1–25

Dear Friend who loves God:[a]

[1,2]Several biographies of Christ have already been written using as their source material the reports circulating among us from the early disciples and other eyewitnesses. [3]However, it occurred to me that it would be well to recheck all these accounts from first to last and after thorough investigation to pass this summary on to you,[b] [4]to reassure you of the truth of all you were taught.

[5]My story begins with a Jewish priest, Zacharias, who lived when Herod was king of Judea. Zacharias was a member of the Abijah division of the Temple service corps. (His wife Elizabeth was, like himself, a member of the priest tribe of the Jews, a descendant of Aaron.) [6]Zacharias and Eliz-

Herod the Great ruled from 37 to 4 B.C. He was king not only of Judea but of other territories as well.

Aaron was the brother of Moses and his descendants made up the priestly class of Israel.

e. Literally, "grace." f. See Mt 17:2 g. Or, "his unique Son."

a. From verse 3. Literally, "most excellent Theophilus." The name means "one who loves God." b. Literally, "an account of the things accomplished among us."

abeth were godly folk, careful to obey all of God's laws in spirit as well as in letter. [7]But they had no children, for Elizabeth was barren; and now they were both very old.

[8,9]One day as Zacharias was going about his work in the Temple—for his division was on duty that week—the honor fell to him by lot[c] to enter the inner sanctuary and burn incense before the Lord. [10]Meanwhile, a great crowd stood outside in the Temple court, praying as they always did during that part of the service when the incense was being burned.

[11,12]Zacharias was in the sanctuary when suddenly an angel appeared, standing to the right of the altar of incense! Zacharias was startled and terrified.

[13]But the angel said, "Don't be afraid, Zacharias! For I have come to tell you that God has heard your prayer, and your wife Elizabeth will bear you a son! And you are to name him John. [14]You will both have great joy and gladness at his birth, and many will rejoice with you. [15]For he will be one of the Lord's great men. He must never touch wine or hard liquor—and he will be filled with the Holy Spirit, even from before his birth! [16]And he will persuade many a Jew to turn to the Lord his God. [17]He will be a man of rugged[d] spirit and power like Elijah, the prophet of old; and he will precede the coming of the Messiah, preparing the people for his arrival. He will soften adult hearts to become like little children's, and will change disobedient minds to the wisdom of faith."[e]

[18]Zacharias said to the angel, "But this is impossible! I'm an old man now, and my wife is also well along in years."

[19]Then the angel said, "I am Gabriel! I stand in

Elizabeth was barren as were Sarah, Rebekah, Rachel, the mother of Samson and the mother of Samuel. Their children were born in a special way.

---

c. Probably by throwing dice or something similar—"drawing straws" would be a modern equivalent.
d. Implied. e. Literally, "to turn the hearts of the fathers to the children, and the disobedient to the wisdom of the just."

the very presence of God. It was he who sent me to you with this good news! [20]And now, because you haven't believed me, you are to be stricken silent, unable to speak until the child is born. For my words will certainly come true at the proper time."

[21]Meanwhile the crowds outside were waiting for Zacharias to appear and wondered why he was taking so long. [22]When he finally came out, he couldn't speak to them, and they realized from his gestures that he must have seen a vision in the Temple. [23]He stayed on at the Temple for the remaining days of his Temple duties and then returned home. [24]Soon afterwards Elizabeth his wife became pregnant and went into seclusion for five months.

[25]"How kind the Lord is," she exclaimed, "to take away my disgrace of having no children!"

Gabriel in Jewish tradition is one of the seven angels who stand in the presence of God. He is mentioned in Dan. 8:16, 9:21.

The Angel Gabriel Announces the Birth of Jesus
Lk 1:26–38

[26]The following month God sent the angel Gabriel to Nazareth, a village in Galilee, [27]to a virgin, Mary, engaged to be married to a man named Joseph, a descendant of King David.

[28]Gabriel appeared to her and said, "Congratulations, favored lady! The Lord is with you!"[f]

[29]Confused and disturbed, Mary tried to think what the angel could mean.

[30]"Don't be frightened, Mary," the angel told her, "for God has decided to wonderfully bless you! [31]Very soon now, you will become pregnant and have a baby boy, and you are to name him 'Jesus.' [32]He shall be very great and shall be called the Son of God. And the Lord God shall give him

Luke is the main source for knowledge about Christ's youth. He tells us (1:4) that he made great efforts to check out his facts.

---

f. Some ancient versions add, "Blessed are you among women," as in verse 42 which appears in all the manuscripts.

the throne of his ancestor David. [33]And he shall reign over Israel forever; his Kingdom shall never end!"

[34]Mary asked the angel, "But how can I have a baby? I am a virgin."

[35]The angel replied, "The Holy Spirit shall come upon you, and the power of God shall over-shadow you; so the baby born to you will be utterly holy—the Son of God. [36]Furthermore, six months ago your Aunt[g] Elizabeth—'the barren one,' they called her—became pregnant in her old age! [37]For every promise from God shall surely come true."

[38]Mary said, "I am the Lord's servant, and I am willing to do whatever he wants. May everything you said come true." And then the angel disappeared.

Mary Visits Elizabeth
Lk 1:39–56

[39,40]A few days later Mary hurried to the highlands of Judea to the town where Zacharias lived, to visit Elizabeth.

Tradition names the town as Ain Karim, five miles west of Jerusalem. The trip would take four days.

[41]At the sound of Mary's greeting, Elizabeth's child leaped within her and she was filled with the Holy Spirit.

[42]She gave a glad cry and exclaimed to Mary, "You are favored by God above all other women, and your child is destined for God's mightiest praise. [43]What an honor this is, that the mother of my Lord should visit me! [44]When you came in and greeted me, the instant I heard your voice, my baby moved in me for joy! [45]You believed that God would do what he said; that is why he has given you this wonderful blessing."

[46]Mary responded, "Oh, how I praise the Lord.

g. Literally, "relative."

⁴⁷How I rejoice in God my Savior! ⁴⁸For he took notice of his lowly servant girl, and now generation after generation forever shall call me blest of God. ⁴⁹For he, the mighty Holy One, has done great things to me. ⁵⁰His mercy goes on from generation to generation, to all who reverence him.

⁵¹"How powerful is his mighty arm! How he scatters the proud and haughty ones! ⁵²He has torn princes from their thrones and exalted the lowly. ⁵³He has satisfied the hungry hearts and sent the rich away with empty hands. ⁵⁴And how he has helped his servant Israel! He has not forgotten his promise to be merciful. ⁵⁵For he promised our fathers—Abraham and his children—to be merciful to them, forever."

⁵⁶Mary stayed with Elizabeth about three months and then went back to her own home.

The Birth of John
Lk 1:57–80

⁵⁷By now Elizabeth's waiting was over, for the time had come for the baby to be born—and it was a boy. ⁵⁸The word spread quickly to her neighbors and relatives of how kind the Lord had been to her, and everyone rejoiced.

⁵⁹When the baby was eight days old, all the relatives and friends came for the circumcision ceremony. They all assumed the baby's name would be Zacharias, after his father.

⁶⁰But Elizabeth said, "No! He must be named John!"

⁶¹"What?" they exclaimed. "There is no one in all your family by that name." ⁶²So they asked the baby's father, talking to him by gestures.ʰ

Jewish law prescribed that a male child be circumcised on the eighth day after his birth. He was named on that day and there was a feast of celebration.

---

h. Zacharias was apparently stone deaf as well as speechless, and had not heard what his wife had said.

⁶³He motioned for a piece of paper and to everyone's surprise wrote, "His name is *John!*" ⁶⁴Instantly Zacharias could speak again, and he began praising God.

⁶⁵Wonder fell upon the whole neighborhood, and the news of what had happened spread through the Judean hills. ⁶⁶And everyone who heard about it thought long thoughts and asked, "I wonder what this child will turn out to be? For the hand of the Lord is surely upon him in some special way."

⁶⁷Then his father Zacharias was filled with the Holy Spirit and gave his prophecy:

⁶⁸"Praise the Lord, the God of Israel, for he has come to visit his people and has redeemed them. ⁶⁹He is sending us a Mighty Savior from the royal line of his servant David, ⁷⁰just as he promised through his holy prophets long ago— ⁷¹someone to save us from our enemies, from all who hate us.

⁷²,⁷³"He has been merciful to our ancestors, yes, to Abraham himself, by remembering his sacred promise to him, ⁷⁴and by granting us the privilege of serving God fearlessly, freed from our enemies, ⁷⁵and by making us holy and acceptable, ready to stand in his presence forever.

⁷⁶"And you, my little son, shall be called the prophet of the glorious God, for you will prepare the way for the Messiah. ⁷⁷You will tell his people how to find salvation through forgiveness of their sins. ⁷⁸And this will be because the mercy of our God is very tender, and heaven's dawn is about to break upon us, ⁷⁹to give light to those who sit in darkness and death's shadow, and to guide us to the path of peace."

⁸⁰The little boy greatly loved God[i] and when he grew up he lived out in the lonely wilderness until he began his public ministry to Israel.

---

i. Literally, "became strong in spirit."

Joseph's Dream
Mt 1:18-25

[18]These are the facts concerning the birth of Jesus Christ: His mother, Mary, was engaged to be married to Joseph. But while she was still a virgin she became pregnant by the Holy Spirit. [19]Then Joseph, her fiance,[b] being a man of stern principle,[c] decided to break the engagement but to do it quietly, as he didn't want to publicly disgrace her.

[20]As he lay awake[d] considering this, he fell into a dream, and saw an angel standing beside him. "Joseph, son of David," the angel said, "don't hesitate to take Mary as your wife! For the child within her has been conceived by the Holy Spirit. [21]And she will have a Son, and you shall name him Jesus (meaning 'Savior'), for he will save his people from their sins. [22]This will fulfill God's message through his prophets—

[23]*'Listen! The virgin shall conceive a child!* She shall give birth to a Son, and he shall be called "Emmanuel" (meaning "God is with us").' "

[24]When Joseph awoke, he did as the angel commanded, and brought Mary home to be his wife, [25]but she remained a virgin until her Son was born; and Joseph named him "Jesus."

In Jewish law a man may adopt a boy by declaring him his son. Also by Jewish law, ancestry is traced through the father. Thus Jesus is of the line of David.

The text is from Is. 7:14.

Jesus Is Born in Bethlehem
Lk 2:1-7

[1]About this time Caesar Augustus, the Roman Emperor, decreed that a census should be taken throughout the nation. [2](This census was taken when Quirinius was governor of Syria.)

[3]Everyone was required to return to his ances-

b. Literally, "her husband." c. Literally, "a just man." d. Implied in remainder of verse.

tral home for this registration. ⁴And because Joseph was a member of the royal line, he had to go to Bethlehem in Judea, King David's ancient home—journeying there from the Galilean village of Nazareth. ⁵He took with him Mary, his fiancee, who was obviously pregnant by this time.

The distance from Nazareth to Bethlehem is about ninety miles, a good four days of travel.

⁶And while they were there, the time came for her baby to be born; ⁷and she gave birth to her first child, a son. She wrapped him in a blanket[a] and laid him in a manger, because there was no room for them in the village inn.

The Shepherds Adore
Lk 2:8–20

⁸That night some shepherds were in the fields outside the village, guarding their flocks of sheep. ⁹Suddenly an angel appeared among them, and the landscape shone bright with the glory of the Lord. They were badly frightened, ¹⁰but the angel reassured them.

"Don't be afraid!" he said. "I bring you the most joyful news ever announced, and it is for everyone! ¹¹The Savior—yes, the Messiah, the Lord—has been born tonight in Bethlehem![b] ¹²How will you recognize him? You will find a baby wrapped in a blanket,[c] lying in a manger!"

¹³Suddenly, the angel was joined by a vast host of others—the armies of heaven—praising God:

¹⁴"Glory to God in the highest heaven," they sang,[d] "and peace on earth for all those pleasing him."

¹⁵When this great army of angels had returned again to heaven, the shepherds said to each other, "Come on! Let's go to Bethlehem! Let's see this wonderful thing that has happened, which the Lord has told us about."

a. Literally, "swaddling clothes."   b. Literally, "in the City of David."   c. Literally, "swaddling clothes."
d. Literally, "said."

16They ran to the village and found their way to Mary and Joseph. And there was the baby, lying in the manger. 17The shepherds told everyone what had happened and what the angel had said to them about this child. 18All who heard the shepherds' story expressed astonishment, 19but Mary quietly treasured these things in her heart and often thought about them.

20Then the shepherds went back again to their fields and flocks, praising God for the visit of the angels, and because they had seen the child, just as the angel had told them.

The Circumcision
Lk 2:21

21Eight days later, at the baby's circumcision ceremony, he was named Jesus, the name given him by the angel before he was even conceived.

The name Jesus means "Yahweh is salvation."

The Presentation
Lk 2:22–38

22When the time came for Mary's purification offering at the Temple, as required by the laws of Moses after the birth of a child, his parents took him to Jerusalem to present him to the Lord; 23for in these laws God had said, "If a woman's first child is a boy, he shall be dedicated to the Lord."

24At that time Jesus' parents also offered their sacrifice for purification—"either a pair of turtledoves or two young pigeons" was the legal requirement. 25That day a man named Simeon, a

According to Lev. 12:2–4, a mother was purified forty days after the birth of a son. The offering for a poor woman was two pigeons.

Jerusalem resident, was in the Temple. He was a good man, very devout, filled with the Holy Spirit and constantly expecting the Messiah[e] to come soon. [26]For the Holy Spirit had revealed to him that he would not die until he had seen him—God's anointed King. [27]The Holy Spirit had impelled him to go to the Temple that day; and so, when Mary and Joseph arrived to present the baby Jesus to the Lord in obedience to the law, [28]Simeon was there and took the child in his arms, praising God.

[29,30,31]"Lord," he said, "now I can die content! For I have seen him as you promised me I would. I have seen the Savior you have given to the world. [32]He is the Light that will shine upon the nations, and he will be the glory of your people Israel!"

[33]Joseph and Mary just stood there, marveling at what was being said about Jesus.

[34,35]Simeon blessed them but then said to Mary, "A sword shall pierce your soul, for this child shall be rejected by many in Israel, and this to their undoing. But he will be the greatest joy of many others. And the deepest thoughts of many hearts shall be revealed."

[36,37]Anna, a prophetess, was also there in the Temple that day. She was the daughter of Phanuel, of the Jewish tribe of Asher, and was very old, for she had been a widow for eighty-four years following seven years of marriage. She never left the Temple but stayed there night and day, worshiping God by praying and often fasting.

[38]She came along just as Simeon was talking with Mary and Joseph, and she also began thanking God and telling everyone in Jerusalem who had been awaiting the coming of the Savior[f] that the Messiah had finally arrived.

---

e. Literally, "the Consolation of Israel."   f. Literally, looking for the redemption of Jerusalem."

The Royal Genealogy
Mt 1:1–17 (Lk 3:23–28)

¹These are the ancestors of Jesus Christ, a descendant of King David and of Abraham:

²Abraham was the father of Isaac; Isaac was the father of Jacob; Jacob was the father of Judah and his brothers.

³Judah was the father of Perez and Zerah (Tamar was their mother); Perez was the father of Hezron; Hezron was the father of Aram;

⁴Aram was the father of Amminadab; Amminadab was the father of Nahshon; Nahshon was the father of Salmon;

⁵Salmon was the father of Boaz (Rahab was his mother); Boaz was the father of Obed (Ruth was his mother); Obed was the father of Jesse;

⁶Jesse was the father of King David. David was the father of Solomon (his mother was the widow of Uriah);

⁷Solomon was the father of Rehoboam; Rehoboam was the father of Abijah; Abijah was the father of Asa;

⁸Asa was the father of Jehoshaphat; Jehoshaphat was the father of Joram; Joram was the father of Uzziah;

⁹Uzziah was the father of Jotham; Jotham was the father of Ahaz; Ahaz was the father of Hezekiah;

¹⁰Hezekiah was the father of Manasseh; Manasseh was the father of Amos; Amos was the father of Josiah;

¹¹Josiah was the father of Jechoniah and his brothers (born at the time of the exile to Babylon).

¹²After the exile: Jechoniah was the father of Shealtiel; Shealtiel was the father of Zerubbabel;

¹³Zerubbabel was the father of Abiud; Abiud

The two genealogies differ. Matthew has forty-two names, Luke seventy-seven. Matthew traces the royal line to Abraham to show Jesus is the savior of the Chosen People. Luke, more universalist, traces Jesus to Adam to show Him as savior of mankind.

was the father of Eliakim; Eliakim was the father of Azor;

¹⁴Azor was the father of Zadok; Zadok was the father of Achim; Achim was the father of Eliud;

¹⁵Eliud was the father of Eleazar; Eleazar was the father of Matthan; Matthan was the father of Jacob;

¹⁶Jacob was the father of Joseph (who was the husband of Mary, the mother of Jesus Christ the Messiah).

¹⁷These are[a] fourteen of the generations from Abraham to King David; and fourteen from King David's time to the exile; and fourteen from the exile to Christ.

The Visit of the Magi
Mt 2:1–12

¹Jesus was born in the town of Bethlehem, in Judea, during the reign of King Herod.

At about that time some astrologers from eastern lands arrived in Jerusalem, asking, ²"Where is the newborn King of the Jews? For we have seen his star in far-off eastern lands, and have come to worship him."

³King Herod was deeply disturbed by their question, and all Jerusalem was filled with rumors.[a] ⁴He called a meeting of the Jewish religious leaders.

"Did the prophets tell us where the Messiah would be born?" he asked.

⁵"Yes, in Bethlehem," they said, "for this is what the prophet Micah[b] wrote:

⁶'O little town of Bethlehem, you are not just an unimportant Judean village, for a Governor shall

The point of this incident is to show the recognition of Jesus by Gentiles. Bethlehem, the home of King David, lies six miles south of Jerusalem. Herod's paranoia about rivals led to the murder of his wife, brother and three sons.

a. Literally, "So all the generations from Abraham unto David are fourteen."
a. Literally, "and all Jerusalem with him." b. Implied. Mi 5:2.

rise from you to rule my people Israel.'"

⁷Then Herod sent a private message to the astrologers, asking them to come to see him; at this meeting he found out from them the exact time when they first saw the star. Then he told them, ⁸"Go to Bethlehem and search for the child. And when you find him, come back and tell me so that I can go and worship him too!"

⁹After this interview the astrologers started out again. And look! The star appeared to them again, standing over Bethlehem.ᶜ ¹⁰Their joy knew no bounds!

¹¹Entering the house where the baby and Mary his mother were, they threw themselves down before him, worshiping. Then they opened their presents and gave him gold, frankincense and myrrh. ¹²But when they returned to their own land, they didn't go through Jerusalem to report to Herod, for God had warned them in a dream to go home another way.

Jesus Becomes a Refugee
Mt 2:13–15

¹³After they were gone, an angel of the Lord appeared to Joseph in a dream. "Get up and flee to Egypt with the baby and his mother," the angel said, "and stay there until I tell you to return, for King Herod is going to try to kill the child." ¹⁴That sameᵈ night he left for Egypt with Mary and the baby, ¹⁵and stayed there until King Herod's death. This fulfilled the prophet's prediction, "I have called my Son from Egypt."ᵉ

There were a number of colonies of Jews in Egypt. The journey would take about a week. Jesus returning to Palestine from Egypt was like a new Moses.

c. Literally, "went before them until it came and stood over where the baby was." d. Implied. e. Hos 11:1

The Murder of the Innocent Children
Mt 2:16–23

¹⁶Herod was furious when he learned that the astrologers had disobeyed him. Sending soldiers to Bethlehem, he ordered them to kill every baby boy two years old and under, both in the town and on the nearby farms, for the astrologers had told him the star first appeared to them two years before. ¹⁷This brutal action of Herod's fulfilled the prophecy of Jeremiah,ᶠ

¹⁸"Screams of anguish come from Ramah,ᵍ
Weeping unrestrained;
Rachel weeping for her children,
Uncomforted—
For they are dead."

¹⁹When Herod died, an angel of the Lord appeared in a dream to Joseph in Egypt, and told him, ²⁰"Get up and take the baby and his mother back to Israel, for those who were trying to kill the child are dead."

²¹So he returned immediately to Israel with Jesus and his mother. ²²But on the way he was frightened to learn that the new king was Herod's son, Archelaus. Then, in another dream, he was warned not to go to Judea, so they went to Galilee instead, ²³and lived in Nazareth. This fulfilled the prediction of the prophets concerning the Messiah, "He shall be called a Nazarene."

The Boyhood of Jesus
Lk 2:40–52

⁴⁰There the child became a strong, robust lad, and was known for wisdom beyond his years; and

---

f. Jeremiah 31:15. g. Or, "the region of Ramah."

God poured out his blessings on him.

[41,42]When Jesus was twelve years old he accompanied his parents to Jerusalem for the annual Passover Festival, which they attended each year. [43]After the celebration was over they started home to Nazareth, but Jesus stayed behind in Jerusalem. His parents didn't miss him the first day, [44]for they assumed he was with friends among the other travelers. But when he didn't show up that evening, they started to look for him among their relatives and friends; [45]and when they couldn't find him, they went back to Jerusalem to search for him there.

[46,47]Three days later they finally discovered him. He was in the Temple, sitting among the teachers of Law, discussing deep questions with them and amazing everyone with his understanding and answers.

[48]His parents didn't know what to think. "Son!" his mother said to him. "Why have you done this to us? Your father and I have been frantic, searching for you everywhere."

[49]"But why did you need to search?" he asked. "Didn't you realize that I would be here at the Temple, in my Father's House?" [50]But they didn't understand what he meant.

[51]Then he returned to Nazareth with them and was obedient to them; and his mother stored away all these things in her heart. [52]So Jesus grew both tall and wise, and was loved by God and man.

The Law prescribed three feasts of pilgrimage to the Temple: Passover, Pentecost and Tabernacles. However, it was the custom for those who lived at a distance to keep only the first.

This is the last mention of Joseph in the Gospels. The opinion is that he died before Jesus began His public life.

2.

THE BEGINNING OF THE MISSION

The Mission of John
Lk 3:1–6, Mt 3:4–6, Lk 3:7–18

[1,2]In the fifteenth year of the reign of Emperor Tiberius Caesar, a message came from God to John (the son of Zacharias), as he was living out in the deserts. (Pilate was governor over Judea at that time; Herod, over Galilee; his brother Philip, over Iturea and Trachonitis; Lysanias, over Abilene; and Annas and Caiaphas were High Priests.) [3]Then John went from place to place on both sides of the Jordan River, preaching that people should be baptized to show that they had turned to God and away from their sins, in order to be forgiven.[a]

[4]In the words of Isaiah the prophet, John was "a voice shouting from the barren wilderness, 'Prepare a road for the Lord to travel on! Widen the pathway before him! [5]Level the mountains! Fill up the valleys! Straighten the curves! Smooth out the ruts! [6]And then all mankind shall see the Savior sent from God.'"

[4]John's clothing was woven from camel's hair and he wore a leather belt; his food was locusts and wild honey. [5]People from Jerusalem and from all over the Jordan Valley, and, in fact, from every section of Judea went out to the wilderness to hear

Luke goes to lengths to date John's mission because it also dates the public life of Jesus. The time would be somewhere in the years of A.D. 27–28.

The text is Is 40:3–4.

a. Or, "preaching the baptism of repentance for remission of sins."

him preach, ⁶and when they confessed their sins, he baptized them in the Jordan River.

⁷Here is a sample of John's preaching to the crowds that came for baptism: "You brood of snakes! You are trying to escape hell without truly turning to God! That is why you want to be baptized! ⁸First go and prove by the way you live that you really have repented. And don't think you are safe because you are descendants of Abraham. That isn't enough. God can produce children of Abraham from these desert stones! ⁹The axe of his judgment is poised over you, ready to sever your roots and cut you down. Yes, every tree that does not produce good fruit will be chopped down and thrown into the fire."

¹⁰The crowd replied, "What do you want us to do?"

¹¹"If you have two coats," he replied, "give one to the poor. If you have extra food, give it away to those who are hungry."

¹²Even tax collectors—notorious for their corruption—came to be baptized and asked, "How shall we prove to you that we have abandoned our sins?"

¹³"By your honesty," he replied. "Make sure you collect no more taxes than the Romanᵇ government requires you to."

¹⁴"And us," asked some soldiers, "what about us?"

John replied, "Don't extort money by threats and violence; don't accuse anyone of what you know he didn't do; and be content with your pay!"

¹⁵Everyone was expecting the Messiah to come soon, and eager to know whether or not John was he. This was the question of the hour, and was being discussed everywhere.

¹⁶John answered the question by saying, "I bap-

b. Implied.

tize only with water; but someone is coming soon who has far higher authority than mine; in fact, I am not even worthy of being his slave.[c] He will baptize you with fire—with the Holy Spirit. [17]He will separate chaff from grain, and burn up the chaff with eternal fire and store away the grain." [18]He used many such warnings as he announced the Good News to the people.

The Baptism of Jesus
Mt 3:13–17, Jn 1:15–18

[13]Then Jesus went from Galilee to the Jordan River to be baptized there by John. [14]John didn't want to do it.

"This isn't proper," he said. "I am the one who needs to be baptized by you."

[15]But Jesus said, "Please do it, for I must do all that is right."[i] So then John baptized him.

[16]After his baptism, as soon as Jesus came up out of the water, the heavens were opened to him and he saw the Spirit of God coming down in the form of a dove. [17]And a voice from heaven said, "This is my beloved Son, and I am wonderfully pleased with him."

[15]John pointed him out to the people, telling the crowds, "This is the one I was talking about when I said, 'Someone is coming who is greater by far than I am—for he existed long before I did!'" [16]We have all benefited from the rich blessings he brought to us—blessing upon blessing heaped upon us! [17]For Moses gave us only the Law with its rigid demands and merciless justice, while Jesus Christ brought us loving forgiveness as well. [18]No one has ever actually seen God, but, of

c. Literally, "of loosing (the sandal strap of) his shoe."

course, his only Son has, for he is the companion of the Father and has told us all about him.

Jesus Is Tempted in the Wilderness
Mt 4:1–11

¹Then Jesus was led out into the wilderness by the Holy Spirit, to be tempted there by Satan. ²For forty days and forty nights he ate nothing and became very hungry. ³Then Satan tempted him to get food by changing stones into loaves of bread.

"It will prove you are the Son of God," he said.

⁴But Jesus told him, "No! For the Scriptures tell us that bread won't feed men's souls: obedience to every word of God is what we need."

⁵Then Satan took him to Jerusalem to the roof of the Temple. ⁶"Jump off," he said, "and prove you are the Son of God; for the Scriptures declare, 'God will send his angels to keep you from harm,' ...they will prevent you from smashing on the rocks below."

⁷Jesus retorted, "It also says not to put the Lord your God to a foolish test!"

⁸Next Satan took him to the peak of a very high mountain and showed him the nations of the world and all their glory. ⁹"I'll give it all to you," he said, "if you will only kneel and worship me."

¹⁰"Get out of here, Satan, " Jesus told him. "The Scriptures say, 'Worship only the Lord God. Obey only him.'"

¹¹Then Satan went away, and angels came and cared for Jesus.

The forty days in the wilderness symbolizes Israel's forty years of testing in the desert lands.

The Testimony of John
Jn 1:19–34

¹⁹The Jewish leaders[h] sent priests and assistant

---

h. Literally, "the Jews."

priests from Jerusalem to ask John whether he claimed to be the Messiah.

²⁰He denied it flatly. "I am not the Christ," he said.

²¹"Well then, who are you?" they asked. "Are you Elijah?"

"No," he replied.

"Are you the Prophet?"ⁱ

"No."

²²"Then who are you? Tell us, so we can give an answer to those who sent us. What do you have to say for yourself?"

²³He replied, "I am a voice from the barren wilderness, shouting as Isaiah prophesied, 'Get ready for the coming of the Lord!'"

²⁴,²⁵Then those who were sent by the Pharisees asked him, "If you aren't the Messiah or Elijah or the Prophet, what right do you have to baptize?"

²⁶John told them, "I merely baptize withʲ water, but right here in the crowd is someone you have never met, ²⁷who will soon begin his ministry among you, and I am not even fit to be his slave."

²⁸This incident took place at Bethany, a village on the other side of the Jordan River where John was baptizing.

²⁹The next day John saw Jesus coming toward him and said, "Look! There is the Lamb of God who takes away the world's sin! ³⁰He is the one I was talking about when I said, 'Soon a man far greater than I am is coming, who existed long before me!' ³¹I didn't know he was the one, but I am here baptizing withʲ water in order to point him out to the nation of Israel."

³²Then John told about seeing the Holy Spirit in the form of a dove descending from heaven and resting upon Jesus.

³³"I didn't know he was the one," John said

It was Jewish belief that Elijah would return to prepare the way for the Messiah. For "the Prophet" see Dt 18:15–17.

i. See Dt 18:15. j. Or, "in."

again, "but at the time God sent me to baptize he told me, 'When you see the Holy Spirit descending and resting upon someone—he is the one you are looking for. He is the one who baptizes with[j] the Holy Spirit.' ³⁴I saw it happen to this man, and I therefore testify that he is the Son of God."

Andrew Brings Peter to Jesus
Jn 1:35–42

³⁵The following day as John was standing with two of his disciples, ³⁶Jesus walked by. John looked at him intently and then declared, "See! There is the Lamb of God!"

³⁷Then John's two disciples turned and followed Jesus.

³⁸Jesus looked around and saw them following. "What do you want?" he asked them.

"Sir," they replied, "where do you live?"

³⁹"Come and see," he said. So they went with him to the place where he was staying and were with him from about four o'clock that afternoon until the evening. ⁴⁰(One of these men was Andrew, Simon Peter's brother.)

⁴¹Andrew then went to find his brother Peter and told him, "We have found the Messiah!" ⁴²And he brought Peter to meet Jesus.

Jesus looked intently at Peter for a moment and then said, "You are Simon, John's son— but you shall be called Peter, the rock!"

The name Jesus gave Peter was in Aramaic, *Kepha*, Rock. Peter is the Greek rendering of that word.

Philip and Nathanael
Jn 1:43–51

⁴³The next day Jesus decided to go to Galilee. He

j. Or "in."

found Philip and told him, "Come with me." [44](Philip was from Bethsaida, Andrew and Peter's home town.)

[45]Philip now went off to look for Nathanael and told him, "We have found the Messiah!—the very person Moses and the prophets told about! His name is Jesus, the son of Joseph from Nazareth!"

[46]"Nazareth!" exclaimed Nathanael. "Can anything good come from there?"

"Just come and see for yourself," Philip declared.

[47]As they approached, Jesus said, "Here comes an honest man—a true son of Israel."

[48]"How do you know what I am like?" Nathanael demanded.

And Jesus replied, "I could see you under the fig tree before Philip found you."

[49]Nathanael replied, "Sir, you are the Son of God—the King of Israel!"

[50]Jesus asked him, "Do you believe all this just because I told you I had seen you under the fig tree? You will see greater proofs than this. [51]You will even see heaven open and the angels of God coming back and forth to me, the Messiah."[k]

Bethsaida was at the north end of the Sea of Galilee where the Jordan River entered the lake. Nathanael is mentioned only by John. He is usually identified with the Apostle, Bartholomew (son of Tholmai).

The Miracle at Cana
Jn 2:1–12

[1]Two days later Jesus' mother was a guest at a wedding in the village of Cana in Galilee, [2]and Jesus and his disciples were invited too. [3]The wine supply ran out during the festivities, and Jesus' mother came to him with the problem.

[4]"I can't help you now," he said.[a] "It isn't yet my time for miracles."

Cana (Kefr Kenna) is identified as a village four miles northeast of Nazareth.

k. Literally, "the Son of Man."   a. Literally, "Woman, what have I to do with you?"

⁵But his mother told the servants, "Do whatever he tells you to."

⁶Six stone waterpots were standing there; they were used for Jewish ceremonial purposes and held perhaps twenty to thirty gallons each. ⁷,⁸Then Jesus told the servants to fill them to the brim with water. When this was done he said, "Dip some out and take it to the master of ceremonies."

⁹When the master of ceremonies tasted the water that was now wine, not knowing where it had come from (though, of course, the servants did), he called the bridegroom over.

¹⁰"This is wonderful stuff!" he said. "You're different from most. Usually a host uses the best wine first, and afterwards, when everyone is full and doesn't care, then he brings out the less expensive brands. But you have kept the best for the last!"

¹¹This miracle at Cana in Galilee was Jesus' first public demonstration of his heaven-sent power. And his disciples believed that he really was the Messiah.ᵇ

¹²After the wedding he left for Capernaum for a few days with his mother, brothers, and disciples.

Capernaum at the northwest end of the Sea of Galilee was almost a second home to Jesus. It appears frequently in the Gospels.

Jesus Goes to Jerusalem
Jn 2:13, 23–25

¹³Then it was time for the annual Jewish Passover celebration, and Jesus went to Jerusalem.

²³Because of the miracles he did in Jerusalem at the Passover celebration, many people were convinced that he was indeed the Messiah. ²⁴,²⁵But Jesus didn't trust them, for he knew mankind to the core. No one needed to tell him how changeable human nature is!

b. Literally, "His disciples believed on him."

Nicodemus Comes by Night
Jn 3:1–22

1,2 After dark one night a Jewish religious leader named Nicodemus, a member of the sect of the Pharisees, came for an interview with Jesus. "Sir," he said, "we all know that God has sent you to teach us. Your miracles are proof enough of this."

3Jesus replied, "With all the earnestness I possess I tell you this: Unless you are born again, you can never get into the Kingdom of God."

4"Born again!" exclaimed Nicodemus. "What do you mean? How can an old man go back into his mother's womb and be born again?"

5Jesus replied, "What I am telling you so earnestly is this: Unless one is born of water[a] and the Spirit, he cannot enter the Kingdom of God. **6**Men can only reproduce human life, but the Holy Spirit gives new life from heaven; **7**so don't be surprised at my statement that you must be born again! **8**Just as you can hear the wind but can't tell where it comes from or where it will go next, so it is with the Spirit. We do not know on whom he will next bestow this life from heaven."

9"What do you mean?" Nicodemus asked.

10,11 Jesus replied, "You, a respected Jewish teacher, and yet you don't understand these things? I am telling you what I know and have seen—and yet you won't believe me. **12**But if you don't even believe me when I tell you about such things as these that happen here among men, how can you possibly believe if I tell you what is going on in heaven? **13**For only I, the Messiah,[b] have come to earth and will return to heaven again. **14**And as Moses in the wilderness lifted up the bronze image of a serpent on a pole, even so I

Nicodemus was a Pharisee and a member of the Sanhedrin. High-class Jews often used Greek names. He comes timidly at night so as not to be seen.

a. Or, "Physical birth is not enough. You must also be born spiritually . . . ." This alternate paraphrase interprets "born of water" as meaning the normal process observed during every human birth. Some think this means water baptism.   b. Literally, "the Son of Man."

must be lifted up upon a pole, ¹⁵so that anyone who believes in me will have eternal life. ¹⁶For God loved the world so much that he gave his only^c Son so that anyone who believes in him shall not perish but have eternal life. ¹⁷God did not send his Son into the world to condemn it, but to save it.

¹⁸"There is no eternal doom awaiting those who trust him to save them. But those who don't trust him have already been tried and condemned for not believing in the only^c Son of God. ¹⁹Their sentence is based on this fact: that the Light from heaven came into the world, but they loved the darkness more than the Light, for their deeds were evil. ²⁰They hated the heavenly Light because they wanted to sin in the darkness. They stayed away from that Light for fear their sins would be exposed and they would be punished. ²¹But those doing right come gladly to the Light to let everyone see that they are doing what God wants them to."

²²Afterwards Jesus and his disciples left Jerusalem and stayed for a while in Judea and baptized there.

John Defends Jesus
Jn 3:23–36

^{23,24}At this time John the Baptist was not yet in prison. He was baptizing at Aenon, near Salim, because there was plenty of water there. ²⁵One day someone began an argument with John's disciples, telling them that Jesus' baptism was best.^d ²⁶So they came to John and said, "Master, the man you met on the other side of the Jordan River—the one you said was the Messiah—he is baptizing

This site has not been identified.

c. Or, "the unique Son of God."   d. Literally, "about purification."

too, and everybody is going over there instead of coming here to us."

²⁷John replied, "God in heaven appoints each man's work. ²⁸My work is to prepare the way for that man so that everyone will go to him. You yourselves know how plainly I told you that I am not the Messiah. I am here to prepare the way for him— that is all. ²⁹The crowds will naturally go to the main attraction^e—the bride will go where the bridegroom is! A bridegroom's friends rejoice with him. I am the Bridegroom's friend, and I am filled with joy at his success. ³⁰He must become greater and greater, and I must become less and less.

³¹"He has come from heaven and is greater than anyone else. I am of the earth, and my understanding is limited to the things of earth. ³²He tells what he has seen and heard, but how few believe what he tells them! ^{33,34}Those who believe him discover that God is a fountain of truth. For this one—sent by God—speaks God's words, for God's Spirit is upon him without measure or limit. ³⁵The Father loves this man because he is his Son, and God has given him everything there is. ³⁶And all who trust him—God's Son—to save them have eternal life; those who don't believe and obey him shall never see heaven, but the wrath of God remains upon them."

Jesus and the Woman at the Well
Jn 4:1–3, Lk 3:19–20, Jn 4:4–45

^{1,2}When the Lord knew that the Pharisees had heard about the greater crowds coming to him than to John to be baptized and to become his disciples—(though Jesus himself didn't baptize them, but his disciples did)— ³he left Judea and

e. Implied.

returned to the province of Galilee.

¹⁹,²⁰(But after John had publicly criticized Herod, governor of Galilee, for marrying Herodias, his brother's wife, and for many other wrongs he had done, Herod put John in prison, thus adding this sin to all his many others.)

⁴He had to go through Samaria on the way, ⁵,⁶and around noon as he approached the village of Sychar, he came to Jacob's Well, located on the parcel of ground Jacob gave to his son Joseph. Jesus was tired from the long walk in the hot sun and sat wearily beside the well.

⁷Soon a Samaritan woman came to draw water, and Jesus asked her for a drink. ⁸He was alone at the time as his disciples had gone into the village to buy some food. ⁹The woman was surprised that a Jew would ask a "despised Samaritan" for anything—usually they wouldn't even speak to them!—and she remarked about this to Jesus.

¹⁰He replied, "If you only knew what a wonderful gift God has for you, and who I am, you would ask me for some *living* water!"

¹¹"But you don't have a rope or a bucket," she said, "and this is a very deep well! Where would you get this living water? ¹²And besides, are you greater than our ancestor Jacob? How can you offer better water than this which he and his sons and cattle enjoyed?"

¹³Jesus replied that people soon became thirsty again after drinking this water. ¹⁴"But the water I give them," he said, "becomes a perpetual spring within them, watering them forever with eternal life."

¹⁵"Please, sir," the woman said, "give me some of that water! Then I'll never be thirsty again and won't have to make this long trip out here every day."

There was mutual hatred between the Samaritans and the Jews. The Samaritans looked upon the Jews as interlopers while the Jews considered the Samaritans schismatics and idolaters.

16"Go and get your husband,   Jesus told her.

17,18"But I'm not married," the woman replied.

"All too true!" Jesus said. "For you have had five husbands, and you aren't even married to the man you're living with now."

19"Sir," the woman said, "you must be a prophet. 20But say, tell me, why is it that you Jews insist that Jerusalem is the only place of worship, while we Samaritans claim it is here [at Mount Gerazim[a]], where our ancestors worshiped?"

21-24Jesus replied, "The time is coming, ma'am, when we will no longer be concerned about whether to worship the Father here or in Jerusalem. For it's not *where* we worship that counts, but *how* we worship—is our worship spiritual and real? Do we have the Holy Spirit's help? For God is Spirit, and we must have his help to worship as we should. The Father wants this kind of worship from us. But you Samaritans know so little about him, worshiping blindly, while we Jews know all about him, for salvation comes to the world through the Jews."

25The woman said, "Well, at least I know that the Messiah will come—the one they call Christ—and when he does, he will explain everything to us."

26Then Jesus told her, "I am the Messiah!"

27Just then his disciples arrived. They were surprised to find him talking to a woman, but none of them asked him why, or what they had been discussing.

28,29Then the woman left her waterpot beside the well and went back to the village and told everyone. "Come and meet a man who told me everything I ever did! Can this be the Messiah?" 30So the people came streaming from the village to see him.

31Meanwhile, the disciples were urging Jesus to

Jesus was not bothered by Jewish scruples. The Jews considered both Samaritans and their drinking utensils unclean. Moreover, a rabbi would never speak to a woman in public.

a. Implied.

eat. ³²"No," he said, "I have some food you don't know about."

³³"Who brought it to him?" the disciples asked each other.

³⁴Then Jesus explained: "My nourishment comes from doing the will of God who sent me, and from finishing his work. ³⁵Do you think the work of harvesting will not begin until the summer ends four months from now? Look around you! Vast fields of human souls are ripening all around us, and are ready now for reaping. ³⁶The reapers will be paid good wages and will be gathering eternal souls into the granaries of heaven! What joys await the sower and the reaper, both together! ³⁷For it is true that one sows and someone else reaps. ³⁸I sent you to reap where you didn't sow; others did the work, and you received the harvest."

³⁹Many from the Samaritan village believed he was the Messiah because of the woman's report: "He told me everything I ever did!" ⁴⁰,⁴¹When they came out to see him at the well, they begged him to stay at their village; and he did, for two days, long enough for many of them to believe in him after hearing him. ⁴²Then they said to the woman, "Now we believe because we have heard him ourselves, not just because of what you told us. He is indeed the Savior of the world."

⁴³,⁴⁴At the end of the two days' stay he went on to Galilee. Jesus used to say, "A prophet is honored everywhere except in his own country!" ⁴⁵But the Galileans welcomed him with open arms, for they had been in Jerusalem at the Passover celebration and had seen some of his miracles.ᵇ

b. See Jn 2:23.

Cure of the Nobleman's Son
Jn 4:46–54

46,47In the course of his journey through Galilee he arrived at the town of Cana, where he had turned the water into wine. While he was there, a man in the city of Capernaum, a governmental official, whose son was very sick, heard that Jesus had come from Judea and was traveling in Galilee. This man went over to Cana, found Jesus, and begged him to come to Capernaum with him and heal his son, who was now at death's door.

48Jesus asked, "Won't any of you believe in me unless I do more and more miracles?"

49The official pled, "Sir, please come now before my child dies."

50Then Jesus told him, "Go back home. Your son is healed!" And the man believed Jesus and started home. 51While he was on his way, some of his servants met him with the news that all was well—his son had recovered. 52He asked them when the lad had begun to feel better, and they replied, "Yesterday afternoon at about one o'clock his fever suddenly disappeared!" 53Then the father realized it was the same moment that Jesus had told him, "Your son is healed." And the officer and his entire household believed that Jesus was the Messiah.

54This was Jesus' second miracle in Galilee after coming from Judea.

Some early commentators identify the official with the centurion of Mt 8:5–13. Some modern commentators think he might be Chuza, Herod's steward in Lk 8:3.

The Return to Nazareth
Lk 4:16–30

16When he came to the village of Nazareth, his boyhood home, he went as usual to the synagogue on Saturday, and stood up to read the Scriptures. [17]The book of Isaiah the prophet was handed to him, and he opened it to the place where it says:

[18,19]"The Spirit of the Lord is upon me; he has appointed me to preach Good News to the poor; he has sent me to heal the brokenhearted and to announce that captives shall be released and the blind shall see, that the downtrodden shall be freed from their oppressors, and that God is ready to give blessings to all who come to him."[b]

[20]He closed the book and handed it back to the attendant and sat down, while everyone in the synagogue gazed at him intently. [21]Then he added, "These Scriptures came true today!"

[22]All who were there spoke well of him and were amazed by the beautiful words that fell from his lips. "How can this be?" they asked. "Isn't this Joseph's son?"

[23]Then he said, "Probably you will quote me that proverb, 'Physician, heal yourself'—meaning, 'Why don't you do miracles here in your home town like those you did in Capernaum?' [24]But I solemnly declare to you that no prophet is accepted in his own home town! [25,26]For example, remember how Elijah the prophet used a miracle to help the widow of Zarephath—a foreigner from the land of Sidon. There were many Jewish widows needing help in those days of famine, for there had been no rain for three and one-half years, and hunger stalked the land; yet Elijah was not sent to them. [27]Or think of the prophet Elisha, who healed Naaman, a Syrian, rather than the many Jewish lepers needing help."

[28]These remarks stung them to fury; [29]and jumping up, they mobbed him and took him to the edge of the hill on which the city was built, to

This is the only reference in the Gospels that Jesus could read and had some education. The scroll would be written in Hebrew and the commentary would be in Aramaic.

b. Literally, "to proclaim the acceptable year of the Lord."

push him over the cliff. [30]But he walked away through the crowd and left them.

Jesus Goes to Capernaum
Mt 4:13–17, Mk 1:15

[13]He left Nazareth and moved to Capernaum, beside the Lake of Galilee, close to Zebulun and Naphtali. [14]This fulfilled Isaiah's prophecy:

[15,16]"The land of Zebulun and the land of Naphtali, beside the Lake, and the countryside beyond the Jordan River, and Upper Galilee where so many foreigners live—there the people who sat in darkness have seen a great Light; they sat in the land of death, and the Light broke through upon them."[b]

[17]From then on, Jesus began to preach.

[15]"At last the time has come!" he announced. "God's Kingdom is near! Turn from your sins and act on this glorious news!"

b. Is 9:1,2.

3.

ORGANIZING THE KINGDOM

Disciples Are Called
Lk 5:1–11

¹One day as he was preaching on the shore of Lake Gennesaret, great crowds pressed in on him to listen to the Word of God. ²He noticed two empty boats standing at the water's edge while the fishermen washed their nets. ³Stepping into one of the boats, Jesus asked Simon, its owner, to push out a little into the water, so that he could sit in the boat and speak to the crowds from there.

⁴When he had finished speaking, he said to Simon, "Now go out where it is deeper and let down your nets and you will catch a lot of fish!"

⁵"Sir," Simon replied, "we worked hard all last night and didn't catch a thing. But if you say so, we'll try again."

⁶And this time their nets were so full that they began to tear! ⁷A shout for help brought their partners in the other boat and soon both boats were filled with fish and on the verge of sinking.

⁸When Simon Peter realized what had happened, he fell to his knees before Jesus and said, "Oh, sir, please leave us—I'm too much of a sinner for you to have around." ⁹For he was awestruck by the size of their catch, as were the others

Lake Gennesaret, Sea of Galilee and Sea of Tiberias are all names for the same lake. It is thirteen miles long and seven miles wide. It is 680 feet below sea level.

with him, [10]and his partners too—James and John, the sons of Zebedee. Jesus replied, "Don't be afraid! From now on you'll be fishing for the souls of men!"

[11]And as soon as they landed, they left everything and went with him.

Preaching in the Synagogue
Mk 1:21–28

[21]Jesus and his companions now arrived at the town of Capernaum and on Saturday morning went into the Jewish place of worship—the synagogue—where he preached. [22]The congregation was surprised at his sermon because he spoke as an authority, and didn't try to prove his points by quoting others—quite unilke what they were used to hearing![i]

[23]A man possessed by a demon was present and began shouting, [24]"Why are you bothering us, Jesus of Nazareth—have you come to destroy us demons? I know who you are—the holy Son of God!"

[25]Jesus curtly commanded the demon to say no more and to come out of the man. [26]At that the evil spirit screamed and convulsed the man violently and left him. [27]Amazement gripped the audience and they began discussing what had happened.

"What sort of new religion is this?" they asked excitedly. "Why, even evil spirits obey his orders!"

[28]The news of what he had done spread quickly through that entire area of Galilee.

Cure of Peter's Mother-in-Law
Mk 1:29–38

[29,30]Then, leaving the synagogue, he and his disci-

---

i. Literally, "not as the scribes."

ples went over to Simon and Andrew's home, where they found Simon's mother-in-law sick in bed with a high fever. They told Jesus about her right away. ³¹He went to her bedside, and as he took her by the hand and helped her to sit up, the fever suddenly left, and she got up and prepared dinner for them!

³²,³³By sunset the courtyard was filled with the sick and demon-possessed, brought to him for healing; and a huge crowd of people from all over the city of Capernaum gathered outside the door to watch. ³⁴So Jesus healed great numbers of sick folk that evening and ordered many demons to come out of their victims. (But he refused to allow the demons to speak, because they knew who he was.)

³⁵The next morning he was up long before day-break and went out alone into the wilderness to pray.

³⁶,³⁷Later, Simon and the others went out to find him, and told him, "Everyone is asking for you."

³⁸But he replied, "We must go on to other towns as well, and give my message to them too, for that is why I came."

Cure of a Leper
Mk 1:39–45

³⁹So he traveled throughout the province of Galilee, preaching in the synogogues and releasing many from the power of demons. ⁴⁰Once a leper came and knelt in front of him and begged to be healed. "If you want to, you can make me well again," he pled.

⁴¹And Jesus, moved with pity, touched him and said, "I want to! Be healed!" ⁴²Immediately the leprosy was gone—the man was healed!

⁴³,⁴⁴Jesus then told him sternly, "Go and be examined immediately by the Jewish priest. Don't stop to speak to anyone along the way. Take along the offering prescribed by Moses for a leper who is healed, so that everyone will have proof that you are well again."

⁴⁵But as the man went on his way he began to shout the good news that he was healed; as a result, such throngs soon surrounded Jesus that he couldn't publicly enter a city anywhere, but had to stay out in the barren wastelands. And people from everywhere came to him there.

Back at Capernaum
Mk 2:1–12

¹Several days later he returned to Capernaum, and the news of his arrival spread quickly through the city. ²Soon the house where he was staying was so packed with visitors that there wasn't room for a single person more, not even outside the door. And he preached the Word to them. ³Four men arrived carrying a paralyzed man on a stretcher. ⁴They couldn't get to Jesus through the crowd, so they dug through the clay roof above his head and lowered the sick man on his stretcher, right down in front of Jesus.ᵃ

⁵When Jesus saw how strongly they believed that he would help, Jesus said to the sick man, "Son, your sins are forgiven!"

⁶But some of the Jewish religious leadersᵇ said to themselves as they sat there, ⁷"What? This is blasphemy! Does he think he is God? For ony God can forgive sins."

⁸Jesus could read their minds and said to them at once, "Why does this bother you? ⁹,¹⁰,¹¹I, the

---

a. Implied. b. Literally, "scribes."

Messiah,[c] have the authority on earth to forgive sins. But talk is cheap—anybody could say that. So I'll prove it to you by healing this man." **Then, turning to the paralyzed man, he commanded,** "Pick up your stretcher and go on home, for you are healed!"[a]

¹²The man jumped up, took the stretcher, and pushed his way through the stunned onlookers! Then how they praised God. "We've never seen anything like this before!" they all exclaimed.

Call of Matthew
Mk 2:13–17

¹³Then Jesus went out to the seashore again, and preached to the crowds that gathered around him. ¹⁴As he was walking up the beach he saw Levi, the son of Alphaeus, sitting at his tax collection booth. "Come with me," Jesus told him. "Come be my disciple."

And Levi jumped to his feet and went along.

¹⁵That night Levi invited his fellow tax collectors and many other notorious sinners to be his dinner guests so that they could meet Jesus and his disciples. (There were many men of this type among the crowds that followed him.) ¹⁶But when some of the Jewish religious leaders[d] saw him eating with these men of ill repute, they said to his disciples, "How can he stand it, to eat with such scum?"

¹⁷When Jesus heard what they were saying, he told them, "Sick people need the doctor, not healthy ones! I haven't come to tell good people to repent, but the bad ones."

Matthew and Levi are the same person. Matthew's account is Mt 9:9-13.

c. Literally, "Son of Man."   a. Implied.

d. Literally, "the scribes of the Pharisees."

Jesus on Fasting
Mk 2:18–28

¹⁸John's disciples and the Jewish leaders some-times fasted, that is, went without food as part of their religion. One day some people came to Jesus and asked why his disciples didn't do this too.

¹⁹Jesus replied, "Do friends of the bridegroom refuse to eat at the wedding feast? Should they be sad while he is with them? ²⁰But some day he will be taken away from them, and then they will mourn. ²¹[Besides, going without food is part of the old way of doing things.ᵃ] It is like patching an old garment with unshrunk cloth! What happens? The patch pulls away and leaves the hole worse than before. ²²You know better than to put new wine into old wineskins. They would burst. The wine would be spilled out and the wineskins ruined. New wine needs fresh wineskins."

²³Another time, on a Sabbath day as Jesus and his disciples were walking through the fields, the disciples were breaking off heads of wheat and eating the grain.ᵉ

²⁴Some of the Jewish religious leaders said to Jesus, "They shouldn't be doing that! It's against our laws to work by harvesting grain on the Sabbath."

²⁵,²⁶But Jesus replied, "Didn't you ever hear about the time King David and his companions were hungry, and he went into the house of God —Abiathar was High Priest then—and they ate the special breadᶠ only priests were allowed to eat? That was against the law too. ²⁷But the Sabbath was made to benefit man, and not man to benefit the Sabbath. ²⁸And I, the Messiah,ᵍ have authority even to decide what men can do on Sabbath days!"

a. Implied.   e. Implied.   f. Literally, "shewbread."   g. Literally, "the Son of Man."

Man with a Deformed Hand
Mk 3:1–12, Mt 12:17–21

¹While in Capernaum Jesus went over to the synagogue again, and noticed a man there with a deformed hand.

²Since it was the Sabbath, Jesus' enemies watched him closely. Would he heal the man's hand? If he did, they planned to arrest him!

³Jesus asked the man to come and stand in front of the congregation. ⁴Then turning to his enemies he asked, "Is it all right to do kind deeds on Sabbath days? Or is this a day for doing harm? Is it a day to save lives or to destroy them?" But they wouldn't answer him. ⁵Looking around at them angrily, for he was deeply disturbed by their indifference to human need, he said to the man, "Reach out your hand." He did, and instantly his hand was healed!

⁶At once the Pharisees went away and met with the Herodians[b] to discuss plans for killing Jesus. ⁷,⁸Meanwhile, Jesus and his disciples withdrew to the beach, followed by a huge crowd from all over Galilee, Judea, Jerusalem, Idumea, from beyond the Jordan River, and even from as far away as Tyre and Sidon. For the news about his miracles had spread far and wide and vast numbers came to see him for themselves.

⁹He instructed his disciples to bring around a boat and to have it standing ready to rescue him in case he was crowded off the beach. ¹⁰For there had been many healings that day and as a result great numbers of sick people were crowding around him, trying to touch him.

¹¹And whenever those possessed by demons caught sight of him they would fall down before him shrieking, "You are the Son of God!" ¹²But he

b. A pro-Roman political party.

strictly warned them not to make him known.

[17]This fulfilled the prophecy of Isaiah concerning him:

[18]"Look at my Servant. See my Chosen One. He is my Beloved, in whom my soul delights. I will put my Spirit upon him, and he will judge the nations. [19]He does not fight nor shout; he does not raise his voice! [20]He does not crush the weak, or quench the smallest hope; he will end all conflict with his final victory, [21]and his name shall be the hope of all the world."

The passage is Is 42:1-4.

The Apostles Appointed
Lk 6:12-13, Mt 10:2-4

[12]One day soon afterwards he went out into the mountains to pray, and prayed all night. [13]At daybreak he called together his followers and chose twelve of them to be the inner circle of his disciples. (They were appointed as his "apostles," or "missionaries.")[2,3,4] Here are their names:

  Simon (also called Peter),
  Andrew (Peter's brother),
  James (Zebedee's son),
  John (James' brother),
  Philip,
  Bartholomew,
  Thomas,
  Matthew (the tax collector),
  James (Alphaeus' son),
  Thaddaeus,
  Simon (a member of "The Zealots," a subversive political party),
  Judas Iscariot (the one who betrayed him).

The lists of the three synoptic authors do not jibe. Jesus did give new names, e.g. Peter. It is thought that Nathanael and Bartholomew are the same man, as are Judas and Thaddeus, and Levi and Matthew.

4.

THE SERMON ON THE MOUNT

The Sermon on the Mount
Lk 6:17–20

17,18 When they came down the slopes of the mountains, they stood with Jesus on a large, level area, surrounded by many of his followers who, in turn, were surrounded by the crowds. For people from all over Judea and from Jerusalem and from as far north as the seacoasts of Tyre and Sidon had come to hear him or to be healed. And he cast out many demons. **19**Everyone was trying to touch him, for when they did, healing power went out from him and they were cured.

20Then he turned to his disciples.

The Beatitudes
Mt 5:3–12

3"Humble men are very fortunate!" he told them, "for the Kingdom of Heaven is given to them. **4**Those who mourn are fortunate! for they shall be comforted. **5**The meek and lowly are fortunate! for the whole wide world belongs to them.

6"Happy are those who long to be just and good, for they shall be completely satisfied. **7**Happy are the kind and merciful, for they shall be shown mercy. [8]Happy are those whose hearts are pure, for they shall see God. [9]Happy are those who strive for peace—they shall be called the sons of God. [10]Happy are those who are persecuted because they are good, for the Kingdom of Heaven is theirs.

[11]"When you are reviled and persecuted and lied about because you are my followers—wonderful! [12]Be *happy* about it! Be *very glad!* for a *tremendous reward* awaits you up in heaven. And remember, the ancient prophets were persecuted too."

Salt of the Earth
Mt 5:13–16

[13]"You are the world's seasoning, to make it tolerable. If you lose your flavor, what will happen to the world? And you yourselves will be thrown out and trampled underfoot as worthless. [14]You are the world's light—a city on a hill, glowing in the night for all to see. [15,16]Don't hide your light! Let it shine for all; let your good deeds glow for all to see, so that they will praise your heavenly Father."

Jesus Fulfills the Law
Mt 5:17–20

[17]"Don't misunderstand why I have come—it isn't to cancel the laws of Moses and the warnings of the prophets. No, I came to fulfill them, and to make them all come true. [18]With all the earnestness I have I say: Every law in the Book will continue until its purpose is achieved.[a] [19]And so if anyone breaks the least commandment, and teaches others to, he shall be the least in the Kingdom of

---

a. Literally, "until all things be accomplished."

Heaven. But those who teach God's laws *and obey them* shall be great in the Kingdom of Heaven.

²⁰"But I warn you—unless your goodness[b] is greater than that of the Pharisees and other Jewish leaders, you can't get into the Kingdom of Heaven at all!"

Don't Hold Grudges
Mt 5:21–26

²¹"Under the laws of Moses the rule was, 'If you kill, you must die.' ²²But I have added to that rule,[c] and tell you that if you are only *angry*, even in your own home,[d] you are in danger of judgment! If you call your friend an idiot, you are in danger of being brought before the court. And if you curse him, you are in danger of the fires of hell.[e]

²³"So if you are standing before the altar in the Temple, offering a sacrifice to God, and suddenly remember that a friend has something against you, ²⁴leave your sacrifice there beside the altar and go and apologize and be reconciled to him, and then come and offer your sacrifice to God. ²⁵Come to terms quickly with your enemy before it is too late and he drags you into court and you are thrown into a debtor's cell, ²⁶for you will stay there until you have paid the last penny."

Jewish teachers counted 613 laws in the Pentateuch and classified them between important and less important. Jesus now refers to some of these laws and gives a commentary on them.

Adultery and Divorce
Mt 5:27–32

²⁷"The laws of Moses said, 'You shall not commit adultery.' ²⁸But I say: Anyone who even looks at a woman with lust in his eye has already committed adultery with her in his heart. ²⁹So if your eye—

b. Literally, "righteousness." c. Literally, "But I say." d. Literally, "with your brother." e. Literally, "the hell of fire."

even if it is your best[f] eye!— causes you to lust, gouge it out and throw it away. Better for part of you to be destroyed than for all of you to be cast into hell. [30]And if your hand—even your right hand —causes you to sin, cut if off and throw it away. Better that than find yourself in hell.

[31]"The law of Moses says, 'If anyone wants to be rid of his wife, he can divorce her merely by giving her a letter of dismissal.' [32]But I say that a man who divorces his wife, except for fornication, causes her to commit adultery if she remarries again. And he who marries her commits adultery."

Mark and Luke writing for Gentiles omit this exception.

Do Not Swear
Mt 5:33–37

[33]"Again, the law of Moses says, 'You shall not break your vows to God, but must fulfill them all.' [34]But I say: Don't make any vows! And even to say, 'By heavens!' is a sacred vow to God, for the heavens are God's throne. [35]And if you say 'By the earth!' it is a sacred vow, for the earth is his footstool. And don't swear 'By Jerusalem!' for Jerusalem is the capital of the great King. [36]Don't even swear 'By my head!' for you can't turn one hair white or black. [37]Say just a simple 'Yes, I will' or 'No, I won't.' Your word is enough. To strengthen your promise with a vow shows that something is wrong."

Love Your Enemies
Mt 5:38–48

[38]"The law of Moses says, 'If a man gouges out another's eye, he must pay with his own eye. If a

---

f. Literally, "your right eye."

tooth gets knocked out, knock out the tooth of the one who did it.'ᵍ ³⁹But I say: Don't resist violence! If you are slapped on one cheek, turn the other too. ⁴⁰If you are ordered to court, and your shirt is taken from you, give your coat too. ⁴¹If the military demand that you carry their gear for a mile, carry it two. ⁴²Give to those who ask, and don't turn away from those who want to borrow.

⁴³"There is a saying, 'Love your *friends* and hate your enemies.' ⁴⁴But I say: Love your *enemies!* Pray for those who *persecute* you! ⁴⁵In that way you will be acting as true sons of your Father in heaven. For he gives his sunlight to both the evil and the good, and sends rain on the just and on the unjust too. ⁴⁶If you love only those who love you, what good is that? Even scoundrels do that much. ⁴⁷If you are friendly only to your friends, how are you different from anyone else? Even the heathen do that. ⁴⁸But you are to be perfect, even as your Father in heaven is perfect."

Jesus emphasizes that the New Law goes beyond the Old.

By law a Roman soldier could compel a conquered person to carry his baggage —but only for a mile!

Do Good in Secret
Mt 6:1–4

¹"Take care! Don't do your good deeds publicly, to be admired, for then you will lose the reward from your Father in heaven. ²When you give a gift to a beggar, don't shout about it as the hypocrites do— blowing trumpets in the synagogues and streets to call attention to their acts of charity! I tell you in all earnestness, they have received all the reward they will ever get. ³But when you do a kindness to someone, do it secretly—don't tell your left hand what your right hand is doing. ⁴And your Father who knows all secrets will reward you."

g. Literally, "an eye for an eye and a tooth for a tooth."

Prayer
Mt 6:5–8

5"And now about prayer. When you pray, don't be like the hypocrites who pretend piety by praying publicly on street corners and in the synagogues where everyone can see them. Truly, that is all the reward they will ever get. 6But when you pray, go away by yourself, all alone, and shut the door behind you and pray to your Father secretly, and your Father, who knows your secrets, will reward you.

7,8"Don't recite the same prayer over and over as the heathen do, who think prayers are answered only by repeating them again and again. Remember, your Father knows exactly what you need even before you ask him!"

Fasting
Mt 6:16–18

16"And now about fasting. When you fast, declining your food for a spiritual purpose, don't do it publicly, as the hypocrites do, who try to look wan and disheveled so people will feel sorry for them. Truly, that is the only reward they will ever get. 17But when you fast, put on festive clothing, 18so that no one will suspect you are hungry, except your Father who knows every secret. And he will reward you."

Trust in God
Mt 6:19–34

19"Don't store up treasures here on earth where

they can erode away or may be stolen. [20]Store them in heaven where they will never lose their value, and are safe from thieves. [21]If your profits are in heaven your heart will be there too.

[22]"If your eye is pure, there will be sunshine in your soul. [23]But if your eye is clouded with evil thoughts and desires, you are in deep spiritual darkness. And oh, how deep that darkness can be!

[24]"You cannot serve two masters: God and money. For you will hate one and love the other, or else the other way around.

[25]"So my counsel is: Don't worry about *things*— food, drink, and clothes. For you already have life and a body—and they are far more important than what to eat and wear. [26]Look at the birds! They don't worry about what to eat—they don't need to sow or reap or store up food—for your heavenly Father feeds them. And you are far more valuable to him than they are. [27]Will all your worries add a single moment to your life?

[28]"And why worry about your clothes? Look at the field lilies! They don't worry about theirs. [29]Yet King Solomon in all his glory was not clothed as beautifully as they. [30]And if God cares so wonderfully for flowers that are here today and gone tomorrow, won't he more surely care for you, O men of little faith?

[31,32]"So don't worry at all about having enough food and clothing. Why be like the heathen? For they take pride in all these things and are deeply concerned about them. But your heavenly Father already knows perfectly well that you need them, [33]and he will give them to you if you give him first place in your life and live as he wants you to.

[34]"So don't be anxious about tomorrow. God will take care of your tomorrow too. Live one day at a time.[b]"

---

b. Literally, "sufficient unto the day is the evil thereof."

Rules for Living
Mt 7:1–29

[1]"Don't criticize, and then you won't be criticized. [2]For others will treat you as you treat them. [3]And why worry about a speck in the eye of a brother when you have a board in your own? [4]Should you say, 'Friend, let me help you get that speck out of your eye,' when you can't even see because of the board in your own? [5]Hypocrite! First get rid of the board. Then you can see to help your brother.

[6]"Don't give holy things to depraved men. Don't give pearls to swine! They will trample the pearls and turn and attack you.

[7]"Ask, and you will be given what you ask for. Seek, and you will find. Knock, and the door will be opened. [8]For everyone who asks, receives. Anyone who seeks, finds. If only you will knock, the door will open. [9]If a child asks his father for a loaf of bread, will he be given a stone instead? [10]If he asks for fish, will he be given a poisonous snake? Of course not! [11]And if you hardhearted, sinful men know how to give good gifts to your children, won't your Father in heaven even more certainly give good gifts to those who ask him for them?

[12]"Do for others what you want them to do for you. This is the teaching of the laws of Moses in a nutshell.[a]

[13]"Heaven can be entered only through the narrow gate! The highway to hell[b] is broad, and its gate is wide enough for all the multitudes who choose its easy way. [14]But the Gateway to Life is small, and the road is narrow, and only a few ever find it.

[15]"Beware of false teachers who come disguised as harmless sheep, but are wolves and will tear

---

a. Literally, "this is the law and the prophets." b. Literally, "the way that leads to destruction."

73

you apart. [16]You can detect them by the way they act, just as you can identify a tree by its fruit. You need never confuse grapevines with thorn bushes or figs with thistles. [17]Different kinds of fruit trees can quickly be identified by examining their fruit. [18]A variety that produces delicious fruit never produces an inedible kind. And a tree producing an inedible kind can't produce what is good. [19]So the trees having the inedible fruit are chopped down and thrown on the fire. [20]Yes, the way to identify a tree or a person[c] is by the kind of fruit produced.

[21]"Not all who sound religious are really godly people. They may refer to me as 'Lord,' but still won't get to heaven. For the decisive question is whether they obey my Father in heaven. [22]At the Judgment[d] many will tell me, 'Lord, Lord, we told others about you and used your name to cast out demons and to do many other great miracles.' [23]But I will reply, 'You have never been mine.[e] Go away, for your deeds are evil.'

[24]"All who listen to my instructions and follow them are wise, like a man who builds his house on solid rock. [25]Though the rain comes in torrents, and the floods rise and the storm winds beat against his house, it won't collapse, for it is built on rock.

[26]"But those who hear my instructions and ignore them are foolish, like a man who builds his house on sand. [27]For when the rains and floods come, and storm winds beat against his house, it will fall with a mighty crash." [28]The crowds were amazed at Jesus' sermons, [29]for he taught as one who had great authority, and not as their Jewish leaders.[f]

---

c. Implied.   d. Literally, "in that day."   e. Literally, "I never knew you."   f. Literally, "not as the scribes." These leaders only quoted others, and did not presume to present any fresh revelation.

5.

THE GALILEAN MINISTRY

Cure of the Army Captain's Slave
Lk 7:1–10

¹When Jesus had finished his sermon he went back into the city of Capernaum.

²Just at that time the highly prized slave of a Roman[a] army captain was sick and near death. ³When the captain heard about Jesus, he sent some respected Jewish elders to ask him to come and heal his slave. ⁴So they began pleading earnestly with Jesus to come with them and help the man. They told him what a wonderful person the captain was.

"If anyone deserves your help, it is he," they said, ⁵"for he loves the Jews and even paid personally to build us a synagogue!"

⁶,⁷,⁸Jesus went with them; but just before arriving at the house, the captain sent some friends to say, "Sir, don't inconvenience yourself by coming to my home, for I am not worthy of any such honor or even to come and meet you. Just speak a word from where you are, and my servant boy will be healed! I know, because I am under the authority of my superior officers, and I have authority over my men. I only need to say 'Go!' and they go; or 'Come!' and they come; and to my

a. Implied.

slave, 'Do this or that,' and he does it. So just say, 'Be healed!' and my servant will be well again!"

⁹Jesus was amazed. Turning to the crowd he said, "Never among all the Jews in Israel have I met a man with faith like this."

¹⁰And when the captain's friends returned to his house, they found the slave completely healed.

The Widow's Dead Son
Lk 7:11–17

¹¹Not long afterwards Jesus went with his disciples to the village of Nain, with the usual great crowd at his heels. ¹²A funeral procession was coming out as he approached the village gate. The boy who had died was the only son of his widowed mother, and many mourners from the village were with her.

This incident is peculiar to Luke. Nain lies eight miles southeast of Nazareth.

¹³When the Lord saw her, his heart overflowed with sympathy. "Don't cry!" he said. ¹⁴Then he walked over to the coffin and touched it, and the bearers stopped. "Laddie," he said, "come back to life again."

¹⁵Then the boy sat up and began to talk to those around him! And Jesus gave him back to his mother.

¹⁶A great fear swept the crowd, and they exclaimed with praises to God, "A mighty prophet has risen among us," and, "We have seen the hand of God at work today."

¹⁷The report of what he did that day raced from end to end of Judea and even out across the borders.

John's Disciples Question Jesus
Mt 11:2–3, Lk 7:20–35

[2]John the Baptist, who was now in prison, heard about all the miracles the Messiah was doing, so he sent his disciples to ask Jesus, [3]"Are you really the one we are waiting for, or shall we keep on looking?"

[20,21,22]The two disciples found Jesus while he was curing many sick people of their various diseases—healing the lame and the blind and casting out evil spirits. When they asked him John's question, this was his reply: "Go back to John and tell him all you have seen and heard here today: how those who were blind can see. The lame are walking without a limp. The lepers are completely healed. The deaf can hear again. The dead come back to life. And the poor are hearing the Good News. [23]And tell him, 'Blessed is the one who does not lose his faith in me.'"[c]

According to Isaiah these are the works of the one who will be the Messiah.

[24]After they left, Jesus talked to the crowd about John. "Who is this man you went out into the Judean wilderness to see?" he asked. "Did you find him weak as grass, moved by every breath of wind? [25]Did you find him dressed in expensive clothes? No! Men who live in luxury are found in palaces, not out in the wilderness. [26]But did you find a prophet? Yes! And more than a prophet. [27]He is the one to whom the Scriptures refer when they say, 'Look! I am sending my messenger ahead of you, to prepare the way before you.' [28]In all humanity there is no one greater than John. And yet the least citizen of the Kingdom of God is greater than he."

[29]And all who heard John preach—even the most wicked of them[d]—agreed that God's requirements were right, and they were baptized by

---

c. Literally, "Blessed is he who keeps from stumbling over me." d. Literally, "even the tax collectors"; i.e., the publicans.

him. ³⁰All, that is, except the Pharisees and teachers of Moses' Law. They rejected God's plan for them and refused John's baptism.

³¹"What can I say about such men?" Jesus asked. "With what shall I compare them? ³²They are like a group of children who complain to their friends, 'You don't like it if we play "wedding" and you don't like it if we play "funeral"'!ᵉ ³³For John the Baptist used to go without food and never took a drop of liquor all his life, and you said, 'He must be crazy!'ᶠ ³⁴But I eat my food and drink my wine, and you say, 'What a glutton Jesus is! And he drinks! And has the lowest sort of friends!'ᵍ ³⁵But I am sure you can always justify your inconsistencies.'"ʰ

The Sinful Woman Is Forgiven
Lk 7:36–50

³⁶One of the Pharisees asked Jesus to come to his home for lunch and Jesus accepted the invitation. As they sat down to eat, ³⁷a woman of the streets —a prostitute—heard he was there and brought an exquisite flask filled with expensive perfume. ³⁸Going in, she knelt behind him at his feet, weeping, with her tears falling down upon his feet; and she wiped them off with her hair and kissed them and poured the perfume on them.

This incident is exclusive to Luke. The text gives no reason to suppose this woman was Mary Magdalene or Mary, the sister of Martha.

³⁹When Jesus' host, a Pharisee, saw what was happening and who the woman was, he said to himself, "This proves that Jesus is no prophet, for if God had really sent him, he would know what kind of woman this one is!"

⁴⁰Then Jesus spoke up and answered his thoughts. "Simon," he said to the Pharisee, "I have something to say to you."

e. Literally, "We played the flute for you and you didn't dance; we sang a dirge and you didn't weep." f. Literally, "He has a demon."   g. Literally, "is a friend of tax gatherers and sinners." h. Literally, "but wisdom is justified of all her children."

"All right, Teacher," Simon replied, "go ahead."

⁴¹Then Jesus told him this story: "A man loaned money to two people—$5,000 to one and $500 to the other. ⁴²But neither of them could pay him back, so he kindly forgave them both, letting them keep the money! Which do you suppose loved him most after that?"

⁴³"I suppose the one who had owed him the most," Simon answered.

"Correct," Jesus agreed.

⁴⁴Then he turned to the woman and said to Simon, "Look! See this woman kneeling here! When I entered your home, you didn't bother to offer me water to wash the dust from my feet, but she has washed them with her tears and wiped them with her hair. ⁴⁵You refused me the customary kiss of greeting, but she has kissed my feet again and again from the time I first came in. ⁴⁶You neglected the usual courtesy of olive oil to anoint my head, but she has covered my feet with rare perfume. ⁴⁷Therefore her sins—and they are many—are forgiven, for she loved me much; but one who is forgiven little, shows little love."

⁴⁸And he said to her, "Your sins are forgiven."

⁴⁹Then the men at the table said to themselves, "Who does this man think he is, going around forgiving sins?"

⁵⁰And Jesus said to the woman, "Your faith has saved you; go in peace."

Cure of the Possessed Man
Mk 3:20–21, Mt 12:22–23

²⁰When he returned to the house where he was staying, the crowds began to gather again, and

soon it was so full of visitors that he couldn't even find time to eat. ²¹When his friends heard what was happening they came to try to take him home with them.

"He's out of his mind," they said.

²²Then a demon-possessed man—he was both blind and unable to talk—was brought to Jesus, and Jesus healed him so that he could both speak and see. ²³The crowd was amazed. "Maybe Jesus is the Messiah!"ᵉ they exclaimed.

Jesus Rebukes the Jewish Teachers
Mk 3:22, Lk 11:17–26

²²But the Jewish teachers of religion who had arrived from Jerusalem said, "His trouble is that he's possessed by Satan, king of demons. That's why demons obey him."

¹⁷He knew the thoughts of each of them, so he said, "Any kingdom filled with civil war is doomed; so is a home filled with argument and strife. ¹⁸Therefore, if what you say is true, that Satan is fighting against himself by empowering me to cast out his demons, how can his kingdom survive? ¹⁹And if I am empowered by Satan, what about your own followers? For they cast out demons! Do you think this proves they are possessed by Satan? Ask *them* if you are right! ²⁰But if I am casting out demons because of power from God, it proves that the Kingdom of God has arrived.

²¹"For when Satan,ᶠ strong and fully armed, guards his palace, it is safe—²²until someone stronger and better armed attacks and overcomes him and strips him of his weapons and carries off his belongings.

e. Literally, "the Son of David."
f. Literally, "the Strong."

23"Anyone who is not for me is against me; if he isn't helping me, he is hurting my cause.

24"When a demon is cast out of a man, it goes to the deserts, searching there for rest; but finding none, it returns to the person it left, 25and finds that its former home is all swept and clean.g. 26Then it goes and gets seven other demons more evil than itself, and they all enter the man. And so the poor fellow is seven timesc worse off than he was before."

The Unforgivable Sin
Mk 3:28–30

28"I solemnly declare that any sin of man can be forgiven, even blasphemy against me; 29but blasphemy against the Holy Spirit can never be forgiven. It is an eternal sin."

30He told them this because they were saying he did his miracles by Satan's power [instead of acknowledging it was by the Holy Spirit's powerc].

The Holy Spirit is the channel of God's grace. In denying the Holy Spirit one denies repentance and dies in sin.

"Who Is My Mother?"
Mk 3:31–35, Lk 11:27–28

31,32Now his mother and brothers arrived at the crowded house where he was teaching, and they sent word for him to come out and talk with them. "Your mother and brothers are outside and want to see you," he was told.

33He replied, "Who is my mother? Who are my brothers?" 34Looking at those around him he said, "These are my mother and brothers! 35Anyone who does God's will is my brother, and my sister, and my mother."

No place does the Gospel say these are Mary's children. Some think they are cousins, others children of Joseph by an earlier marriage.

g. But empty, since the person is neutral about Christ.

c. Implied.

²⁷As he was speaking, a woman in the crowd called out, "God bless your mother—the womb from which you came, and the breasts that gave you suck!"

²⁸He replied, "Yes, but even more blessed are all who hear the Word of God and put it into practice."

6.

HE TAUGHT BY PARABLES

The Good Samaritan
Lk 10:25–37

²⁵One day an expert on Moses' laws came to test Jesus' orthodoxy by asking him this question: "Teacher, what does a man need to do to live forever in heaven?"

²⁶Jesus replied, "What does Moses' law say about it?"

²⁷"It says," he replied, "that you must love the Lord your God with all your heart, and with all your soul, and with all your strength, and with all your mind. And you must love your neighbor just as much as you love yourself."

²⁸"Right!" Jesus told him. "*Do* this and *you* shall live!"

²⁹The man wanted to justify (his lack of love for some kinds of people),[d] so he asked, "Which neighbors?"

³⁰Jesus replied with an illustration: "A Jew going on a trip from Jerusalem to Jericho was attacked by bandits. They stripped him of his clothes and money and beat him up and left him lying half dead beside the road.

³¹"By chance a Jewish priest came along; and when he saw the man lying there, he crossed to

The road from Jerusalem to Jericho was an important trade route. It was the road to the Jordan River and the way up the Jordan Valley. One literally went down to Jericho since Jerusalem is twenty-five hundred feet above sea level and Jericho eight hundred feet below.

d. Literally, "wanting to justify himself."

the other side of the road and passed him by. ³²A Jewish Temple-assistant^e walked over and looked at him lying there, but then went on.

³³"But a despised Samaritan^f came along, and when he saw him, he felt deep pity. ³⁴Kneeling beside him the Samaritan soothed his wounds with medicine and bandaged them. Then he put the man on his donkey and walked along beside him till they came to an inn, where he nursed him through the night.^g ³⁵The next day he handed the innkeeper two twenty-dollar bills^h and told him to take care of the man. 'If his bill runs higher than that,' he said, 'I'll pay the difference the next time I am here.'

³⁶"Now which of these three would you say was a neighbor to the bandits' victim?"

³⁷The man replied, "The one who showed him some pity."

Then Jesus said, "Yes, now go and do the same."

Persistent Prayer
Lk 18:1–8

¹One day Jesus told his disciples a story to illustrate their need for constant prayer and to show them that they must keep praying until the answer comes.

²"There was a city judge," he said, "a very godless man who had great contempt for everyone. ³A widow of that city came to him frequently to appeal for justice against a man who had harmed her. ⁴,⁵The judge ignored her for a while, but eventually she got on his nerves.

"'I fear neither God nor man,' he said to himself, 'but this woman bothers me. I'm going to see

e. Literally, "Levite."   f. Literally, "a Samaritan." All Samaritans were despised by Jews, and the feeling was mutual, due to historic reasons.   g. Literally, "took care of him."   h. Literally, "two denarii," each the equivalent of a modern day's wage.

that she gets justice, for she is wearing me out with her constant coming!' "

⁶Then the Lord said, "If even an evil judge can be worn down like that, ⁷don't you think that God will surely give justice to his people who plead with him day and night? ⁸Yes! He will answer them quickly! But the question is: When I, the Messiah,ᵃ return, how many will I find who have faith [and are prayingᵇ]?"

More on Persistent Prayer
Lk 11:5–13

⁵,⁶Then, teaching them more about prayer, he used this illustration: "Suppose you went to a friend's house at midnight, wanting to borrow three loaves of bread. You would shout up to him, 'A friend of mine has just arrived for a visit and I've nothing to give him to eat.' ⁷He would call down from his bedroom, 'Please don't ask me to get up. The door is locked for the night and we are all in bed. I just can't help you this time.'

⁸"But I'll tell you this—though he won't do it as a friend, if you keep knocking long enough he will get up and give you everything you want—just because of your persistence. ⁹And so it is with prayer—keep on asking and you will keep on getting; keep on looking and you will keep on finding; knock and the door will be opened. ¹⁰Everyone who asks, receives; all who seek, find; and the door is opened to everyone who knocks.

¹¹"You men who are fathers—if your boy asks for bread, do you give him a stone? If he asks for fish, do you give him a snake? ¹²If he asks for an egg, do you give him a scorpion? [Of course not!ᶜ]

---

a. Literally, "the Son of Man."   b. Implied.

c. Implied.

[13]"And if even sinful persons like yourselves give children what they need, don't you realize that your heavenly Father will do at least as much, and give the Holy Spirit to those who ask for him?"

Humble Prayer
Lk 18:9–14

[9]Then he told this story to some who boasted of their virtue and scorned everyone else:

[10]"Two men went to the Temple to pray. One was a proud, self-righteous Pharisee, and the other a cheating tax collector. [11]The proud Pharisee 'prayed' this prayer: 'Thank God, I am not a sinner like everyone else, especially like that tax collector over there! For I never cheat, I don't commit adultery, [12]I go without food twice a week, and I give to God a tenth of everything I earn.'

[13]"But the corrupt tax collector stood at a distance and dared not even lift his eyes to heaven as he prayed, but beat upon his chest in sorrow, exclaiming, 'God, be merciful to me, a sinner.' [14]I tell you, this sinner, not the Pharisee, returned home forgiven! For the proud shall be humbled, but the humble shall be honored."

Publicans were tax collectors, often extortioners, who were generally despised because of their actions and the fact that they worked for the Romans.

Trust in God
Lk 12:13–59

[13]Then someone called from the crowd, "Sir, please tell my brother to divide my father's estate with me."

[14]But Jesus replied, "Man, who made me a judge over you to decide such things as that? [15]Beware! Don't always be wishing for what you don't have. For real life and real living are not related to

how rich we are."

16Then he gave an illustration: "A rich man had a fertile farm that produced fine crops. 17In fact, his barns were full to overflowing—he couldn't get everything in. He thought about his problem, 18and finally exclaimed, 'I know— I'll tear down my barns and build bigger one! Then I'll have room enough. 19And I'll sit back and say to myself, "Friend, you have enough stored away for years to come. Now take it easy! Wine, women, and song for you!"'ᶜ

20"But God said to him, 'Fool! Tonight you die. Then who will get it all?'

21"Yes, every man is a fool who gets rich on earth but not in heaven."

22Then turning to his disciples he said, "Don't worry about whether you have enough food to eat or clothes to wear. 23For life consists of far more than food and clothes. 24Look at the ravens—they don't plant or harvest or have barns to store away their food, and yet they get along all right—for God feeds them. And you are far more valuable to him than any birds!

25"And besides, what's the use of worrying? What good does it do? Will it add a single day to your life? Of course not! 26And if worry can't even do such little things as that, what's the use of worrying over bigger things?

27"Look at the lilies! They don't toil and spin, and yet Solomon in all his glory was not robed as well as they are. 28And if God provides clothing for the flowers that are here today and gone tomorrow, don't you suppose that he will provide clothing for you, you doubters? 29And don't worry about food—what to eat and drink; don't worry at all that God will provide it for you. 30All mankind scratches for its daily bread, but your heavenly

c. Literally, "Eat, drink, and be merry."

Father knows your needs. [31]He will always give you all you need from day to day if you will make the Kingdom of God your primary concern.

[32]"So don't be afraid, little flock. For it gives your Father great happiness to give you the Kingdom. [33]Sell what you have and give to those in need. This will fatten your purses in heaven! And the purses of heaven have no rips or holes in them. Your treasures there will never disappear; no thief can steal them; no moth can destroy them. [34]Wherever your treasure is, there your heart and thoughts will also be.

[35]"Be prepared—all dressed and ready—[36]for your Lord's return from the wedding feast. Then you will be ready to open the door and let him in the moment he arrives and knocks. [37]There will be great joy for those who are ready and waiting for his return. He himself will seat them and put on a waiter's uniform and serve them as they sit and eat! [38]He may come at nine o'clock at night—or even at midnight. But whenever he comes there will be joy for his servants who are ready!

[39]"Everyone would be ready for him if they knew the exact hour of his return—just as they would be ready for a thief if they knew when he was coming. [40]So be ready all the time. For I, the Messiah,[d] will come when least expected."

[41]Peter asked, "Lord, are you talking just to us or to everyone?"

[42,43,44]And the Lord replied, "I'm talking to any faithful, sensible man whose master gives him the responsibility of feeding the other servants. If his master returns and finds that he has done a good job, there will be a reward—his master will put him in charge of all he owns.

[45]"But if the man begins to think, 'My Lord won't be back for a long time,' and begins to whip

d. Literally, "the Son of Man."

the men and women he is supposed to protect, and to spend his time at drinking parties and in drunkenness—⁴⁶well, his master will return without notice and remove him from his position of trust and assign him to the place of the unfaithful. ⁴⁷He will be severely punished, for though he knew his duty he refused to do it.

⁴⁸"But anyone who is not aware that he is doing wrong will be punished only lightly. Much is required from those to whom much is given, for their responsibility is greater.

⁴⁹"I have come to bring fire to the earth, and, oh, that my task were completed! ⁵⁰There is a terrible baptism ahead of me, and how I am pent up until it is accomplished!

⁵¹"Do you think I have come to give peace to the earth? *No!* Rather, strife and division! ⁵²From now on families will be split apart, three in favor of me, and two against—or perhaps the other way around. ⁵³A father will decide one way about me; his son, the other; mother and daughter will disagree; and the decision of an honoredᵉ mother-in-law will be spurned by her daughter-in-law."

⁵⁴Then he turned to the crowd and said, "When you see clouds beginning to form in the west, you say, 'Here comes a shower.' And you are right.

⁵⁵"When the south wind blows you say, 'Today will be a scorcher.' And it is. ⁵⁶Hypocrites! You interpret the sky well enough, but you refuse to notice the warnings all around you about the crisis ahead. ⁵⁷Why do you refuse to see for yourselves what is right?

⁵⁸"If you meet your accuser on the way to court, try to settle the matter before it reaches the judge, lest he sentence you to jail; ⁵⁹for if that happens you won't be free again until the last penny is paid in full."

Clouds would come from the Mediterranean Sea to the west. Hot winds came up from the southern desert.

e. Implied by ancient custom.

The Place at Table
Lk 14:7–14

⁷When he noticed that all who came to the dinner were trying to sit near the head of the table, he gave them this advice: ⁸"If you are invited to a wedding feast, don't always head for the best seat. For if someone more respected than you shows up, ⁹the host will bring him over to where you are sitting and say, 'Let this man sit here instead.' And you, embarrassed, will have to take whatever seat is left at the foot of the table!

¹⁰"Do this instead—start at the foot; and when your host sees you he will come and say, 'Friend, we have a better place than this for you!' Thus you will be honored in front of all the other guests. ¹¹For everyone who tries to honor himself shall be humbled; and he who humbles himself shall be honored." ¹²Then he turned to his host. "When you put on a dinner," he said, "don't invite friends, brothers, relatives and rich neighbors! For they will return the invitation. ¹³Instead, invite the poor, the crippled, the lame, and the blind. ¹⁴Then at the resurrection of the godly, God will reward you for inviting those who can't repay you."

Jesus gave this advice at a dinner in the home of a member of the Jewish Supreme Court. The place was probably Jerusalem and the host could have been Nicodemus.

The Invitation Goes to Others
Lk 14:15–24

¹⁵Hearing this, a man sitting at the table with Jesus exclaimed, "What a privilege it would be to get into the Kingdom of God!"

¹⁶Jesus replied with this illustration: "A man prepared a great feast and sent out many invitations. ¹⁷When all was ready, he sent his servant around to notify the guests that it was time for

The rejection of the Kingdom by the Jewish establishment and its opening to the Gentiles was a constant theme of Jesus.

them to arrive. [18]But they all began making excuses. One said he had just bought a field and wanted to inspect it, and asked to be excused. [19]Another said he had just bought five pair of oxen and wanted to try them out. [20]Another had just been married and for that reason couldn't come.

[21]"The servant returned and reported to his master what they had said. His master was angry and told him to go quickly into the streets and alleys of the city and to invite the beggars, crippled, lame, and blind. [22]But even then, there was still room.

[23]"'Well, then,' said his master, 'go out into the country lanes and out behind the hedges and urge anyone you find to come, so that the house will be full. [24]For none of those I invited first will get even the smallest taste of what I had prepared for them.'"

The Cost of Discipleship
Lk 14:25–35

[25]Great crowds were following him. He turned around and addressed them as follows: [26]"Anyone who wants to be my follower must love me far more than[a] he does his own father, mother, wife, children, brothers, or sisters—yes, more than his own life—otherwise he cannot be my disciple. [27]And no one can be my disciple who does not carry his own cross and follow me.

[28]"But don't begin until you count the cost.[b] For who would begin construction of a building without first getting estimates and then checking to see if he has enough money to pay the bills? [29]Otherwise he might complete only the foundation before running out of funds. And then how everyone would laugh!

a. Literally, "If anyone comes to me and does not hate his father and mother...." b. Implied in verse 33.

³⁰"'See that fellow there?' they would mock. 'He started that building and ran out of money before it was finished!'

³¹"Or what king would ever dream of going to war without first sitting down with his counselors and discussing whether his army of 10,000 is strong enough to defeat the 20,000 men who are marching against him?

³²"If the decision is negative, then while the enemy troops are still far away, he will send a truce team to discuss terms of peace. ³³So no one can become my disciple unless he first sits down and counts his blessings—and then renounces them all for me.

³⁴"What good is salt that has lost its saltiness?c ³⁵Flavorless salt is fit for nothing—not even for fertilizer. It is worthless and must be thrown out. Listen well, if you would understand my meaning."

The Lost Sheep
Lk 15:1–10

¹Dishonest tax collectors and other notorious sinners often came to listen to Jesus' sermons; ²but this caused complaints from the Jewish religious leaders and the experts on Jewish law because he was associating with such despicable people— even eating with them! ³,⁴So Jesus used this illustration: "If you had a hundred sheep and one of them strayed away and was lost in the wilderness, wouldn't you leave the ninety-nine others to go and search for the lost one until you found it? ⁵And then you would joyfully carry it home on your shoulders. ⁶When you arrived you would call together your friends and neighbors to rejoice

---

c. Perhaps the reference is to impure salt; when wet, the salt dissolves and drains out, leaving a tasteless residue. Mt 5:13.

with you because your lost sheep was found.

⁷"Well, in the same way heaven will be happier over one lost sinner who returns to God than over ninety-nine others who haven't strayed away!

⁸"Or take another illustration: A woman has ten valuable silver coins and loses one. Won't she light a lamp and look in every corner of the house and sweep every nook and cranny until she finds it? ⁹And then won't she call in her friends and neighbors to rejoice with her? ¹⁰In the same way there is joy in the presence of the angels of God when one sinner repents."

The Prodigal Son
Lk 15:10–32

To further illustrate the point, he told them this story: ¹¹"A man had two sons. ¹²When the younger told his father, 'I want my share of your estate now, instead of waiting until you die!' his father agreed to divide his wealth between his sons.

¹³"A few days later this younger son packed all his belongings and took a trip to a distant land, and there wasted all his money on parties and prostitutes. ¹⁴About the time his money was gone a great famine swept over the land, and he began to starve. ¹⁵He persuaded a local farmer to hire him to feed his pigs. ¹⁶The boy became so hungry that even the pods he was feeding the swine looked good to him. And no one gave him anything.

Pods were the fruit of the carob tree.

¹⁷"When he finally came to his senses, he said to himself, 'At home even the hired men have food enough and to spare, and here I am, dying of hunger! ¹⁸I will go home to my father and say,

"Father, I have sinned against both heaven and you, ¹⁹and am no longer worthy of being called your son. Please take me on as a hired man.'"

²⁰"So he returned home to his father. And while he was still a long distance away, his father saw him coming, and was filled with loving pity and ran and embraced him and kissed him.

²¹"His son said to him, 'Father, I have sinned against heaven and you, and am not worthy of being called your son—'

²²"But his father said to the slaves, 'Quick! Bring the finest robe in the house and put it on him. And a jeweled ring for his finger; and shoes! ²³And kill the calf we have in the fattening pen. We must celebrate with a feast, ²⁴for this son of mine was dead and has returned to life. He was lost and is found.' So the party began.

²⁵"Meanwhile, the older son was in the fields working; when he returned home, he heard dance music coming from the house, ²⁶and he asked one of the servants what was going on.

²⁷" 'Your brother is back' he was told, 'and your father has killed the calf we were fattening and has prepared a great feast to celebrate his coming home again unharmed.'

²⁸"The older brother was angry and wouldn't go in. His father came out and begged him, ²⁹but he replied, 'All these years I've worked hard for you and never once refused to do a single thing you told me to; and in all that time you never gave me even one young goat for a feast with my friends. ³⁰Yet when this son of yours comes back after spending your money on prostitutes, you celebrate by killing the finest calf we have on the place.'

³¹" 'Look, dear son,' his father said to him, 'you

and I are very close, and everything I have is yours. ³²But it is right to celebrate. For he is your brother; and he was dead and has come back to life! He was lost and is found!'"

The Dishonest Accountant
Lk 16:1–18

¹Jesus now told this story to his disciples: "A rich man hired an accountant to handle his affairs, but soon a rumor went around that the accountant was thoroughly dishonest.

²"So his employer called him in and said, 'What's this I hear about your stealing from me? Get your report in order, for you are to be dismissed.'

³"The accountant thought to himself, 'Now what? I'm through here, and I haven't the strength to go out and dig ditches, and I'm too proud to beg. ⁴I know just the thing! And then I'll have plenty of friends to take care of me when I leave!'

⁵,⁶"So he invited each one who owed money to his employer to come and discuss the situation. He asked the first one, 'How much do you owe him?' 'My debt is 850 gallons of olive oil,' the man replied. 'Yes, here is the contract you signed,' the accountant told him. 'Tear it up and write another one for half that much!'

⁷"'And how much do you owe him?' he asked the next man. 'A thousand bushels of wheat,' was the reply. 'Here,' the accountant said, 'take your note and replace it with one for only 800 bushels!'

⁸"The rich man had to admire the rascal for being so shrewd.ᵃ And it is true that the citizens of this world are more clever [in dishonesty!ᵇ] than

a. Or, "Do you think the rich man commended the scoundrel for being so shrewd?"   b. Implied.

the godly[c] are. 9But shall I tell *you* to act that way,
to buy friendship through cheating? Will this en-
sure your entry into an everlasting home in heav-
en?[d] 10*No!*[b] For unless you are honest in small matters, you won't be in large ones. If you cheat even
a little, you won't be honest with greater responsibilities. 11And if you are untrustworthy about
worldly wealth, who will trust you with the true
riches of heaven? 12And if you are not faithful with
other people's money, why should you be entrusted with money of your own?

13"For neither you nor anyone else can serve
two masters. You will hate one and show loyalty
to the other, or else the other way around—you
will be enthusiastic about one and despise the
other. You cannot serve both God and money."

14 The Pharisees, who dearly loved their money,
naturally scoffed at all this.

15**Then he said to them,** "You wear a noble,
pious expression in public, but God knows your
evil hearts. Your pretense brings you honor from
the people, but it is an abomination in the sight of
God. 16Until John the Baptist began to preach, the
laws of Moses and the messages of the prophets
were your guides. But John introduced the Good
News that the Kingdom of God would come
soon. And now eager multitudes are pressing in.
17But that doesn't mean that the Law has lost its
force in even the smallest point. It is as strong and
unshakable as heaven and earth.

18"So anyone who divorces his wife and marries
someone else commits adultery, and anyone who
marries a divorced woman commits adultery."

c. Literally, "sons of the light."   d. Literally, and probably ironically, "Make to yourselves friends by
means of the mammon of unrighteousness; that when it shall fail you, they may receive you into the eternal
tabernacles!" Some commentators would interpret this to mean: "Use your money for good, so that it will
be waiting to befriend you when you get to heaven." But this would imply the end justifies the means, an
unbiblical idea.

The Rich Man and the Beggar
Lk 16:19–31

[19]"There was a certain rich man," **Jesus said,** "who was splendidly clothed and lived each day in mirth and luxury. [20]One day Lazarus, a diseased beggar, was laid at his door. [21]As he lay there longing for scraps from the rich man's table, the dogs would come and lick his open sores. [22]Finally the beggar died and was carried by the angels to be with Abraham in the place of the righteous dead.[e] The rich man also died and was buried, [23]and his soul went into hell.[f] There, in torment, he saw Lazarus in the far distance with Abraham.

> Sheol was the abode of the dead. It had adjoining quarters for the good and evil (Enoch 22).

[24]" 'Father Abraham,' he shouted, 'have some pity! Send Lazarus over here if only to dip the tip of his finger in water and cool my tongue, for I am in anguish in these flames.'

[25]"But Abraham said to him, 'Son, remember that during your lifetime you had everything you wanted, and Lazarus had nothing. So now he is here being comforted and you are in anguish. [26]And besides, there is a great chasm separating us, and anyone wanting to come to you from here is stopped at its edge; and no one over there can cross to us.'

[27]"Then the rich man said, 'O Father Abraham, then please send him to my father's home—[28]for I have five brothers—to warn them about this place of torment lest they come here when they die.'

[29]"But Abraham said, 'The Scriptures have warned them again and again. Your brothers can read them any time they want to.'

[30]"The rich man replied, 'No, Father Abraham, they won't bother to read them. But if someone is sent to them from the dead, then they will turn from their sins.'

---

e. Literally, "into Abraham's bosom." f. Literally, "into Hades."

³¹"But Abraham said, 'If they won't listen to Moses and the prophets, they won't listen even though someone rises from the dead.' "ᵍ

g. Even Christ's resurrection failed to convince the Pharisees, to whom he gave this illustration.

7.

THE KINGDOM PARABLES

The Sower
Mk 4:1–25

¹Once again an immense crowd gathered around him on the beach as he was teaching, so he got into a boat and sat down and talked from there. ²His usual method of teaching was to tell the people stories. One of them went like this:

³"Listen! A farmer decided to sow some grain. As he scattered it across his field, ⁴some of it fell on a path, and the birds came and picked it off the hard ground and ate it. ⁵,⁶Some fell on thin soil with underlying rock. It grew up quickly enough, but soon wilted beneath the hot sun and died because the roots had no nourishment in the shallow soil. ⁷Other seeds fell among thorns that shot up and crowded the young plants so that they produced no grain. ⁸But some of the seeds fell into good soil and yielded thirty times as much as he had planted—some of it even sixty or a hundred times as much! ⁹If you have ears, listen!"

¹⁰Afterwards, when he was alone with the Twelve and with his other disciples, they asked him, "What does your story mean?"

¹¹,¹²He replied, "You are permitted to know some truths about the Kingdom of God that are

hidden to those outside the Kingdom:

'Though they see and hear, they will not understand or turn to God, or be forgiven for their sins.'

13"But if you can't understand *this* simple illustration, what will you do about all the others I am going to tell?

14"The farmer I talked about is anyone who brings God's message to others, trying to plant good seed within their lives. 15The hard pathway, where some of the seed fell, represents the hard hearts of some of those who hear God's message; Satan comes at once to try to make them forget it. 16The rocky soil represents the hearts of those who hear the message with joy, 17but, like young plants in such soil, their roots don't go very deep, and though at first they get along fine, as soon as persecution begins, they wilt.

18"The thorny ground represents the hearts of people who listen to the Good News and receive it, 19but all too quickly the attractions of this world and the delights of wealth, and the search for success and lure of nice things come in and crowd out God's message from their hearts, so that no crop is produced.

20"But the good soil represents the hearts of those who truly accept God's message and produce a plentiful harvest for God—thirty, sixty, or even a hundred times as much as was planted in their hearts." 21Then he asked them, "When someone lights a lamp, does he put a box over it to shut out the light? Of course not! The light couldn't be seen or used. A lamp is placed on a stand to shine and be useful.

22"All that is now hidden will someday come to light. 23If you have ears, listen! 24And be sure to put into practice what you hear. The more you do this, the more you will understand what I tell you.

²⁵To him who has shall be given; from him who has not shall be taken away even what he has.''

The Thistles
Mt 13:24–30, 36–43

²⁴Here is another illustration Jesus used: ''The Kingdom of Heaven is like a farmer sowing good seed in his field; ²⁵but one night as he slept, his enemy came and sowed thistles among the wheat. ²⁶When the crop began to grow, the thistles grew too.

²⁷''The farmer's men came and told him, 'Sir, the field where you planted that choice seed is full of thistles!'

²⁸'''An enemy has done it,' he exclaimed.

'''Shall we pull out the thistles?' they asked.

²⁹'''No,' he replied. 'You'll hurt the wheat if you do. ³⁰Let both grow together until the harvest, and I will tell the reapers to sort out the thistles and burn them, and put the wheat in the barn.''''

³⁶Then, leaving the crowds outside, he went into the house. His disciples asked him to explain to them the illustration of the thistles and the wheat.

³⁷''All right,'' he said, ''I[f] am the farmer who sows the choice seed. ³⁸The field is the world, and the seed represents the people of the Kingdom; the thistles are the people belonging to Satan. ³⁹The enemy who sowed the thistles among the wheat is the devil; the harvest is the end of the world,[g] and the reapers are the angels.

⁴⁰''Just as in this story the thistles are separated and burned, so shall it be at the end of the world:[g] ⁴¹I[f] will send my angels and they will separate out of the Kingdom every temptation and all who are evil, ⁴² and throw them into the furnace and burn

---

f. Literally, ''the Son of Man.'' g. Or, ''age.''

them. There shall be weeping and gnashing of teeth. [43]Then the godly shall shine as the sun in their Father's Kingdom. Let those with ears, listen!"

The Mustard Seed
Mt 13:30–32

[30]Jesus asked, "How can I describe the Kingdom of God? What story shall I use to illustrate it? [31,32]It is like a tiny mustard seed! Though this is one of the smallest of seeds, yet it grows to become one of the largest of plants, with long branches where birds can build their nests and be sheltered."

The Leaven
Mt 13:33

[33]He also used this example:
   "The Kingdom of Heaven can be compared to a woman making bread. She takes a measure of flour and mixes in the yeast until it permeates every part of the dough."

The Hidden Treasure
Mt 13:44

[44]"The Kingdom of Heaven is like a treasure a man discovered in a field. In his excitement, he sold everything he owned to get enough money to buy the field—and get the treasure, too!"

The Pearl of Great Price
Mt 13:44–45

[45]"Again, the Kingdom of Heaven is like a pearl

merchant on the lookout for choice pearls. [46]He discovered a real bargain—a pearl of great value— and sold everything he owned to purchase it!"

The Wedding Banquet
Mt 22:1–14

[1,2]Jesus told several other stories to show what the Kingdom of Heaven is like.

"For instance," he said, "it can be illustrated by the story of a king who prepared a great wedding dinner for his son. [3]Many guests were invited, and when the banquet was ready he sent messengers to notify everyone that it was time to come. But all refused! [4]So he sent other servants to tell them, 'Everything is ready and the roast is in the oven. Hurry!'

[5]"But the guests he had invited merely laughed and went on about their business, one to his farm, another to his store, [6]others beat up his messengers and treated them shamefully, even killing some of them.

[7]"Then the angry king sent out his army and destroyed the murderers and burned their city. [8]And he said to his servants, 'The wedding feast is ready, and the guests I invited aren't worthy of the honor. [9]Now go out to the street corners and invite everyone you see.'

[10]"So the servants did, and brought in all they could find, good and bad alike; and the banquet hall was filled with guests. [11]But when the king came in to meet the guests he noticed a man who wasn't wearing the wedding robe [provided for him[a]].

[12]"'Friend,' he asked, 'how does it happen that you are here without a wedding robe?' And the man had no reply.

Jesus is probably referring to the prophets whose message was not always welcomed and who were persecuted.

a. Implied.

13"Then the king said to his aides, 'Bind him hand and foot and throw him out into the outer darkness where there is weeping and gnashing of teeth.' 14For many are called, but few are chosen.''

The Foolish Bridesmaids
Mt 25:1–13

1"The Kingdom of Heaven can be illustrated by the story of ten bridesmaids[a] who took their lamps and went to meet the bridegroom. 2,3,4But only five of them were wise enough to fill their lamps with oil, while the other five were foolish and forgot.

5,6"So, when the bridegroom was delayed, they lay down to rest until midnight, when they were roused by the shout, 'The bridegroom is coming! Come out and welcome him!'

7,8"All the girls jumped up and trimmed their lamps. Then the five who hadn't any oil begged the others to share with them, for their lamps were going out.

9"But the others replied, 'We haven't enough. Go instead to the shops and buy some for yourselves.'

10"But while they were gone, the bridegroom came, and those who were ready went in with him to the marriage feast, and the door was locked.

11"Later, when the other five returned, they stood outside, calling, 'Sir, open the door for us!'

12"But he called back, 'Go away! It is too late!'[b]

13"So stay awake and be prepared, for you do not know the date or moment of my return.''[c]

a. Literally, "virgins."   b. Literally, "I know you not!"   c. Implied.

The Invested Money
Mt 25:14–30

¹⁴"Again, the Kingdom of Heaven can be illustrated by the story of a man going into another country, who called together his servants and loaned them money to invest for him while he was gone.

¹⁵"He gave $5,000 to one, $2,000 to another, and $1,000 to the last—dividing it in proportion to their abilities—and then left on his trip. ¹⁶The man who received the $5,000 began immediately to buy and sell with it and soon earned another $5,000. ¹⁷The man with $2,000 went right to work, too, and earned another $2,000.

¹⁸"But the man who received the $1,000 dug a hole in the ground and hid the money for safe-keeping.

¹⁹"After a long time their master returned from his trip and called them to him to account for his money. ²⁰The man to whom he had entrusted the $5,000 brought him $10,000.

²¹"His master praised him for good work. 'You have been faithful in handling this small amount,' he told him, 'so now I will give you many more responsibilities. Begin the joyous tasks I have assigned to you.'

²²"Next came the man who had received the $2,000, with the report, 'Sir, you gave me $2,000 to use, and I have doubled it.'

²³"'Good work,' his master said. 'You are a good and faithful servant. You have been faithful over this small amount, so now I will give you much more.'

²⁴,²⁵"Then the man with the $1,000 came and said, 'Sir, I knew you were a hard man, and I was afraid you would rob me of what I earned,ᵈ so I hid

---

d. Literally, "reaping where you didn't sow, and gathering where you didn't scatter, and I was afraid..."

your money in the earth and here it is!'

²⁶"But his master replied, 'Wicked man! Lazy slave! Since you knew I would demand your profit, ²⁷you should at least have put my money into the bank so I could have some interest. ²⁸Take the money from this man and give it to the man with the $10,000. ²⁹For the man who uses well what he is given shall be given more, and he shall have abundance. But from the man who is unfaithful, even what little responsibility he has shall be taken from him. ³⁰And throw the useless servant out into outer darkness: there shall be weeping and gnashing of teeth.'"

The Unjust Debtor
Mt 18:23–35

²³"The Kingdom of Heaven can be compared to a king who decided to bring his accounts up to date. ²⁴In the process, one of his debtors was brought in who owed him $10,000,000!ᵍ ²⁵He couldn't pay, so the king ordered him sold for the debt, also his wife and children and everything he had.

²⁶"But the man fell down before the king, his face in the dust, and said, 'Oh, sir, be patient with me and I will pay it all.'

²⁷"Then the king was filled with pity for him and released him and forgave his debt.

²⁸"But when the man left the king, he went to a man who owed him $2,000ʰ and grabbed him by the throat and demanded instant payment.

²⁹"The man fell down before him and begged him to give him a little time. 'Be patient and I will pay it,' he pled.

³⁰"But his creditor wouldn't wait. He had the man arrested and jailed until the debt would be paid in full.

---

g. Literally, "10,000 talents," approximately £ 3,000,000.   h. Approximately £ 700.

³¹"Then the man's friends went to the king and told him what had happened. ³²And the king called before him the man he had forgiven and said, 'You evil-hearted wretch! Here I forgave you all that tremendous debt, just because you asked me to—³³shouldn't you have mercy on others, just as I had mercy on you?'

³⁴"Then the angry king sent the man to the torture chamber until he had paid every last penny due. ³⁵So shall my heavenly Father do to you if you refuse to truly forgive your brothers."

The Fishing Net
Mt 13:47–52

⁴⁷,⁴⁸"Again, the Kingdom of Heaven can be illustrated by a fisherman—he casts a net into the water and gathers in fish of every kind, valuable and worthless. When the net is full, he drags it up onto the beach and sits down and sorts out the edible ones into crates and throws the others away. ⁴⁹That is the way it will be at the end of the world[h]—the angels will come and separate the wicked people from the godly, ⁵⁰casting the wicked into the fire; there shall be weeping and gnashing of teeth. ⁵¹Do you understand?"

"Yes," they said, "we do."

⁵²Then he added, "Those experts in Jewish law who are now my disciples have double treasures—from the Old Testament as well as from the New!"[i]

The Good Seed
Mk 4:26–29

²⁶"Here is another story illustrating what the

---

h. Or, "age."   i. Literally, "brings back out of his treasure things both new and old." The paraphrase is of course highly anachronistic!

Kingdom of God is like:

"A farmer sowed his field, [27]and went away, and as the days went by, the seeds grew and grew without his help. [28]For the soil made the seeds grow. First a leaf-blade pushed through, and later the wheat-heads formed and finally the grain ripened, [29]and then the farmer came at once with his sickle and harvested it."

Use of Parables Prophesied
Mt 13:34–35

[34,35]Jesus constantly used these illustrations when speaking to the crowds. In fact, because the prophets said that he would use so many, he never spoke to them without at least one illustration. For it had been prophesied, "I will talk in parables; I will explain mysteries hidden since the beginning of time."[e]

e. Ps 78:2.

8.

BUILDING THE KINGDOM

Stilling the Storm
Mk 4:35–41

[35]As evening fell, Jesus said to his disciples, "Let's cross to the other side of the lake." [36]So they took him just as he was and started out, leaving the crowds behind (though other boats followed). [37]But soon a terrible storm arose. High waves began to break into the boat until it was nearly full of water and about to sink. [38]Jesus was asleep at the back of the boat with his head on a cushion. Frantically they wakened him, shouting, "Teacher, don't you even care that we are all about to drown?"

This is one of the miracles done for the benefit of the Apostles.

[39]Then he rebuked the wind and said to the sea, "Quiet down!" And the wind fell, and there was a great calm!

[40]And he asked them, "Why were you so fearful? Don't you even yet have confidence in me?"

[41]And they were filled with awe and said among themselves, "Who is this man, that even the winds and seas obey him?"

The Demon-Possessed Man
Mk 5:1–20

[1,2]When they arrived at the other side of the lake a

demon-possessed man ran out from a graveyard, just as Jesus was climbing from the boat.

3,4This man lived among the gravestones, and had such strength that whenever he was put into handcuffs and shackles—as he often was—he snapped the handcuffs from his wrists and smashed the shackles and walked away. No one was strong enough to control him. 5All day long and through the night he would wander among the tombs and in the wild hills, screaming and cutting himself with sharp pieces of stone.

6When Jesus was still far out on the water, the man had seen him and had run to meet him, and fell down before him.

7,8Then Jesus spoke to the demon within the man and said, "Come out, you evil spirit."

It gave a terrible scream, shrieking, "What are you going to do to me, Jesus, Son of the Most High God? For God's sake, don't torture me!"

9"What is your name?" Jesus asked, and the demon replied, "Legion, for there are many of us here within this man."

10Then the demons begged him again and again not to send them to some distant land.

11Now as it happened there was a huge herd of hogs rooting around on the hill above the lake. 12"Send us into those hogs," the demons begged.

13And Jesus gave them permission. Then the evil spirits came out of the man and entered the hogs, and the entire herd plunged down the steep hillside into the lake and drowned.

14The herdsmen fled to the nearby towns and countryside, spreading the news as they ran. Everyone rushed out to see for themselves. 15And a large crowd soon gathered where Jesus was; but as they saw the man sitting there, fully clothed and perfectly sane, they were frightened. 16Those

The headlong destruction of the swine shows the destructive force of evil. To the Jews it was fitting that unclean spirits should have gone into unclean animals.

who saw what happened were telling everyone about it, [17]and the crowd began pleading with Jesus to go away and leave them alone! [18]So he got back into the boat. The man who had been possessed by the demons begged Jesus to let him go along. [19]But Jesus said no.

"Go home to your friends," he told him, "and tell them what wonderful things God has done for you; and how merciful he has been."

[20]So the man started off to visit the Ten Towns[a] of that region and began to tell everyone about the great things Jesus had done for him; and they were awestruck by his story.

Jairus Begs for Help
Mk 5:21–23

[21]When Jesus had gone across by boat to the other side of the lake, a vast crowd gathered around him on the shore.

[22]The leader of the local synagogue, whose name was Jairus, came and fell down before him, [23]pleading with him to heal his little daughter.

"She is at the point of death," he said in desperation. "Please come and place your hands on her and make her live."

Jairus was an archisynagogos. The synagogue was governed by a council of elders. They elected one of their number to preside. The incident shows even an influential Jew would come to Jesus when in need.

The Woman with a Hemorrhage
Mk 5:24–34

[24]Jesus went with him, and the crowd thronged behind. [25]In the crowd was a woman who had been sick for twelve years with a hemorrhage. [26]She had suffered much from many doctors through the years and had become poor from pay-

---

a. Or, "to visit Decapolis."

ing them, and was no better but, in fact, was worse. ²⁷She had heard all about the wonderful miracles Jesus did, and that is why she came up behind him through the crowd and touched his clothes.

²⁸For she thought to herself, "If I can just touch his clothing, I will be healed." ²⁹And sure enough, as soon as she had touched him, the bleeding stopped and she knew she was well!

³⁰Jesus realized at once that healing power had gone out from him, so he turned around in the crowd and asked, "Who touched my clothes?"

³¹His disciples said to him, "All this crowd pressing around you, and you ask who touched you?"

³²But he kept on looking around to see who it was who had done it. ³³Then the frightened woman, trembling at the realization of what had happened to her, came and fell at his feet and told him what she had done. ³⁴And he said to her, "Daughter, your faith has made you well; go in peace, healed of your disease."

Jairus' Daughter Dies
Mk 5:35–43

³⁵While he was still talking to her, messengers arrived from Jairus' home with the news that it was too late—his daughter was dead and there was no point in Jesus' coming now. ³⁶But Jesus ignored their comments and said to Jairus, "Don't be afraid. Just trust me."

³⁷Then Jesus halted the crowd and wouldn't let anyone go on with him to Jairus' home except Peter and James and John. ³⁸When they arrived, Jesus saw that all was in great confusion, with unrestrained weeping and wailing. ³⁹He went inside and spoke to the people.

Peter, James and John seem to have had a special intimacy with Jesus. They will be with Him at the Transfiguration and at the Agony in the Garden.

"Why all this weeping and commotion?" he asked. "The child isn't dead; she is only asleep!"

⁴⁰They laughed at him in bitter derision, but he told them all to leave, and taking the little girl's father and mother and his three disciples, he went into the room where she was lying.

⁴¹,⁴²Taking her by the hand he said to her, "Get up, little girl!" (She was twelve years old.) And she jumped up and walked around! Her parents just couldn't get over it. ⁴³Jesus instructed them very earnestly not to tell what had happened, and told them to give her something to eat.

Cure of Two Blind Men ·
Mt 9:27–31

²⁷As Jesus was leaving her home, two blind men followed along behind, shouting, "O Son of King David, have mercy on us."

²⁸They went right into the house where he was staying, and Jesus asked them, "Do you believe I can make you see?"

"Yes, Lord," they told him, "we do."

²⁹Then he touched their eyes and said, "Because of your faith it will happen."

³⁰And suddenly they could see! Jesus sternly warned them not to tell anyone about it, ³¹but instead they spread his fame all over the town.ʰ

Cure of the Dumb Man
Mt 9:32–34

³²Leaving that place, Jesus met a man who couldn't speak because a demon was inside him. ³³So Jesus cast out the demon, and instantly the

h. Literally, "in all that land."

man could talk. How the crowds marveled! "Never in all our lives have we seen anything like this," they exclaimed.

³⁴But the Pharisees said, "The reason he can cast out demons is that he is demon-possessed himself —possessed by Satan, the demon king!"

Missioners Are Needed
Mt 9:35-38

³⁵Jesus traveled around through all the cities and villages of that area, teaching in the Jewish synagogues and announcing the Good News about the Kingdom. And wherever he went he healed people of every sort of illness. ³⁶And what pity he felt for the crowds that came, because their problems were so great and they didn't know what to do or where to go for help. They were like sheep without a shepherd.

³⁷"The harvest is so great, and the workers are so few," he told his disciples. ³⁸"So pray to the one in charge of the harvesting, and ask him to recruit more workers for his harvest fields."

Jesus Commissions His Apostles
Mt 10:1, 5-42

¹Jesus called his twelve disciples to him, and gave them authority to cast out evil spirits and to heal every kind of sickness and disease.

⁵Jesus sent them out with these instructions: "Don't go to the Gentiles or the Samaritans, ⁶but only to the people of Israel—God's lost sheep. ⁷Go and announce to them that the Kingdom of Heaven is near.ᵃ ⁸Heal the sick, raise the dead,

Because of the Covenant, the Jews had first call. The mission to the Gentiles came later.

a. Or, "at hand," or "has arrived."

cure the lepers, and cast out demons. Give as freely as you have received!

⁹"Don't take any money with you; ¹⁰don't even carry a duffle bag with extra clothes and shoes, or even a walking stick; for those you help should feed and care for you. ¹¹Whenever you enter a city or village, search for a godly man and stay in his home until you leave for the next town. ¹²When you ask permission to stay, be friendly, ¹³and if it turns out to be a godly home, give it your blessing; if not, keep the blessing. ¹⁴Any city or home that doesn't welcome you—shake off the dust of that place from your feet as you leave. ¹⁵Truly, the wicked cities of Sodom and Gomorrah will be better off at Judgment Day than they.

¹⁶"I am sending you out as sheep among wolves. Be as wary as serpents and harmless as doves. ¹⁷But beware! For you will be arrested and tried, and whipped in the synagogues. ¹⁸Yes, and you must stand trial before governors and kings for my sake. This will give you the opportunity to tell them about me, yes, to witness to the world.

¹⁹"When you are arrested, don't worry about what to say at your trial, for you will be given the right words at the right time. ²⁰For it won't be you doing the talking—it will be the Spirit of your heavenly Father speaking through you!

²¹"Brother shall betray brother to death, and fathers shall betray their own children. And children shall rise against their parents and cause their deaths. ²²Everyone shall hate you because you belong to me. But all of you who endure to the end shall be saved.

²³"When you are persecuted in one city, flee to the next! Iᵇ will return before you have reached them all! ²⁴A student is not greater than his teacher. A servant is not above his master. ²⁵The

b. Literally, "the Son of Man."

student shares his teacher's fate. The servant shares his master's! And since I, the master of the household, have been called 'Satan,'[c] how much more will you! 26But don't be afraid of those who threaten you. For the time is coming when the truth will be revealed: their secret plots will become public information.

27"What I tell you now in the gloom, shout abroad when daybreak comes. What I whisper in your ears, proclaim from the housetops!

28"Don't be afraid of those who can kill only your bodies—but can't touch your souls! Fear only God who can destroy both soul and body in hell. 29Not one sparrow (What do they cost? Two for a penny?) can fall to the ground without your Father knowing it. 30And the very hairs of your head are all numbered. 31So don't worry! You are more valuable to him than many sparrows.

32"If anyone publicly acknowledges me as his friend, I will openly acknowledge him as my friend before my Father in heaven. 33But if anyone publicly denies me, I will openly deny him before my Father in heaven.

34"Don't imagine that I came to bring peace to the earth! No, rather, a sword. 35I have come to set a man against his father, and a daughter against her mother, and a daughter-in-law against her mother-in-law—36a man's worst enemies will be right in his own home! 37If you love your father and mother more than you love me, you are not worthy of being mine; or if you love your son or daughter more than me, you are not worthy of being mine. 38If you refuse to take up your cross and follow me, you are not worthy of being mine.

39"If you cling to your life, you will lose it; but if you give it up for me, you will save it.

c. See Mt 9:34, where they called him this.

⁴⁰"Those who welcome you are welcoming me. And when they welcome me they are welcoming God who sent me. ⁴¹If you welcome a prophet because he is a man of God, you will be given the same reward a prophet gets. And if you welcome good and godly men because of their godliness, you will be given a reward like theirs.

⁴²"And if, as my representatives, you give even a cup of cold water to a little child, you will surely be rewarded."

The Gentile Woman
Mk 7:24-30

²⁴Then he left Galilee and went to the region of Tyre and Sidon,ᵈ and tried to keep it a secret that he was there, but couldn't. For as usual the news of his arrival spread fast.

²⁵Right away a woman came to him whose little girl was possessed by a demon. She had heard about Jesus and now she came and fell at his feet, ²⁶and pled with him to release her child from the demon's control. (But she was Syrophoenician— a "despised Gentile!")

²⁷Jesus told her, "First I should help my own family—the Jews. ᵉIt isn't right to take the children's food and throw it to the dogs."

²⁸She replied, "That's true, sir, but even the puppies under the table are given some scraps from the children's plates."

²⁹"Good!" he said, "You have answered well— so well that I have healed your little girl. Go on home, for the demon has left her!"

³⁰And when she arrived home, her little girl was lying quietly in bed, and the demon was gone.

The only two cures Jesus worked at a distance were for Gentiles—this and the Roman officer's slave (Mt 8:5-13).

d. About fifty miles away.   e. Literally, "Let the children eat first."

117

The Deaf Man
Mk 7:31–37

³¹From Tyre he went to Sidon, then back to the Sea of Galilee by way of the Ten Towns. ³²A deaf man with a speech impediment was brought to him, and everyone begged Jesus to lay his hands on the man and heal him.

³³Jesus led him away from the crowd and put his fingers into the man's ears, then spat and touched the man's tongue with the spittle. ³⁴Then, looking up to heaven, he sighed and commanded, "Open!"³⁵Instantly the man could hear perfectly and speak plainly!

³⁶Jesus told the crowd not to spread the news, but the more he forbade them, the more they made it known, ³⁷for they were overcome with utter amazement. Again and again they said, "Everything he does is wonderful; he even corrects deafness and stammering!"

Tyre and Sidon were on the Mediterranean Sea. The Ten Towns were north of Galilee.

Jesus Feeds Five Thousand
Mk 6:30–44, Jn 6:14–15

³⁰The apostles now returned to Jesus from their tour and told him all they had done and what they had said to the people they visited.

³¹Then Jesus suggested "Let's get away from the crowds for a while and rest."For so many people were coming and going that they scarcely had time to eat. ³²So they left by boat for a quieter spot. ³³But many people saw them leaving and ran on ahead along the shore and met them as they landed. ³⁴So the usual vast crowd was there as he stepped from the boat; and he had pity on them because they were like sheep without a shepherd, and he taught them many things they needed to know.

35,36Late in the afternoon his disciples came to him and said, "Tell the people to go away to the nearby villages and farms and buy themselves some food, for there is nothing to eat here in this desolate spot, and it is getting late."

37But Jesus said, *"You feed them."*

"With what?" they asked. "It would take a fortune[a] to buy food for all this crowd!"

38"How much food do we have?" he asked. "Go and find out."

They came back to report that there were five loaves of bread and two fish. 39,40Then Jesus told the crowd to sit down, and soon colorful groups of fifty or a hundred each were sitting on the green grass.

41He took the five loaves and two fish and looking up to heaven, gave thanks for the food. Breaking the loaves into pieces, he gave some of the bread and fish to each disciple to place before the people. 42And the crowd ate until they could hold no more!

43,44There were about 5,000 men there for that meal, and afterwards twelve basketfuls of scraps were picked up off the grass!

14When the people realized what a great miracle had happened, they exclaimed, "Surely, he is the Prophet we have been expecting!"

15Jesus saw that they were ready to take him by force and make him their king, so he went higher into the mountains alone.

Jesus Walks on the Lake
Jn 6:16–18, Mt 14:25–36

16That evening his disciples went down to the shore to wait for him. 17But as darkness fell and Jesus still had not come back, they got into the

---

a. Literally, "200 denarii," a year's wage.

boat and headed out across the lake toward Capernaum. [18]But soon a gale swept down upon them as they rowed, and the sea grew very rough.

[25]About four o'clock in the morning Jesus came to them, walking on the water! [26]They screamed in terror, for they thought he was a ghost.

[27]But Jesus immediately spoke to them, reassuring them. "Don't be afraid!" he said.

[28]Then Peter called to him: "Sir, if it is really you, tell me to come over to you, walking on the water."

[29]"All right," the Lord said, "come along!"

So Peter went over the side of the boat and walked on the water toward Jesus. [30]But when he looked around at the high waves, he was terrified and began to sink. "Save me, Lord!" he shouted.

[31]Instantly Jesus reached out his hand and rescued him. "O man of little faith," Jesus said. "Why did you doubt me?" [32]And when they had climbed back into the boat, the wind stopped.

[33]The others sat there, awestruck. "You really are the Son of God!" they exclaimed.

[34]They landed at Gennesaret. [35]The news of their arrival spread quickly throughout the city, and soon people were rushing around, telling everyone to bring in their sick to be healed. [36]The sick begged him to let them touch even the tassel of his robe, and all who did were healed.

"I Am the Bread of Life!"
Jn 6:22–71

[22,23]The next morning, back across the lake, crowds began gathering on the shore [waiting to see Jesus[d]]. For they knew that he and his disciples had come over together and that the disciples had gone off in their boat, leaving him behind.

d. Implied.

Several small boats from Tiberias were nearby, ²⁴so when the people saw that Jesus wasn't there, nor his disciples, they got into the boats and went across to Capernaum to look for him.

²⁵When they arrived and found him, they said, "Sir, how did you get here?" ²⁶Jesus replied, "The truth of the matter is that you want to be with me because I fed you, not because you believe in me. ²⁷But you shouldn't be so concerned about perishable things like food. No, spend your energy seeking the eternal life that I, the Messiah,ᵉ can give you. For God the Father has sent me for this very purpose."

²⁸They replied, "What should we do to satisfy God?"

²⁹Jesus told them, "This is the will of God, that you believe in the one he has sent."

³⁰,³¹They replied, "You must show us more miracles if you want us to believe you are the Messiah. Give us free bread every day, like our fathers had while they journeyed through the wilderness! As the Scriptures say, 'Moses gave them bread from heaven.'"

³²Jesus said, "Moses didn't give it to them. My Father did.ᵈ And now he offers you true Bread from heaven. ³³The true Bread is a Person—the one sent by God from heaven, and he gives life to the world."

³⁴"Sir," they said, "give us that bread every day of our lives!"

³⁵Jesus replied, "I am the Bread of Life. No one coming to me will ever be hungry again. Those believing in me will never thirst. ³⁶But the trouble is, as I have told you before, you haven't believed even though you have seen me. ³⁷But some will come to me—those the Father has given me—and I will never, never reject them. ³⁸For I have come

d. Implied. e. Literally, "the Son of Man."

here from heaven to do the will of God who sent me, not to have my own way. ³⁹And this is the will of God, that I should not lose even one of all those he has given me, but that I should raise them to eternal life at the Last Day. ⁴⁰For it is my Father's will that everyone who sees his Son and believes on him should have eternal life—that I should raise him at the Last Day."

⁴¹**Then the Jews began to murmur against him because he claimed to be the Bread from heaven.**

⁴²**"What?" they exclaimed. "Why, he is merely Jesus the son of Joseph, whose father and mother we know. What is this he is saying, that he came down from heaven?"**

⁴³**But Jesus replied,** "Don't murmur among yourselves about my saying that. ⁴⁴For no one can come to me unless the Father who sent me draws him to me, and at the Last Day I will cause all such to rise again from the dead. ⁴⁵As it is written in the Scriptures, 'They shall all be taught of God.' Those the Father speaks to, who learn the truth from him, will be attracted to me. ⁴⁶(Not that anyone actually sees the Father, for only I have seen him.)

⁴⁷"How earnestly I tell you this—anyone who believes in me already has eternal life! ⁴⁸⁻⁵¹Yes, I am the Bread of Life! When your fathers in the wilderness ate bread from the skies, they all died. But the Bread from heaven gives eternal life to everyone who eats it. I am that Living Bread that came down out of heaven. Anyone eating this Bread shall live forever; this Bread is my flesh given to redeem humanity."

⁵²**Then the Jews began arguing with each other about what he meant. "How can this man give us his flesh to eat?" they asked.**

⁵³**So Jesus said it again,** "With all the earnestness I possess I tell you this: Unless you eat the

flesh of the Messiah[f] and drink his blood, you cannot have eternal life within you. [54]But anyone who does eat my flesh and drink my blood has eternal life, and I will raise him at the Last Day. [55]For my flesh is the true food, and my blood is the true drink. [56]Everyone who eats my flesh and drinks my blood is in me, and I in him. [57]I live by the power of the living Father who sent me, and in the same way those who partake of me shall live because of me! [58]I am the true Bread from heaven; and anyone who eats this Bread shall live forever, and not die as your fathers did—though they ate bread from heaven." [59](He preached this sermon in the synagogue in Capernaum.)

[60]Even his disciples said, "This is very hard to understand. Who can tell what he means?"

[61]Jesus knew within himself that his disciples were complaining and said to them, "Does *this* offend you? [62]Then what will you think if you see me, the Messiah,[g] return to heaven again? [63]Only the Holy Spirit gives eternal life.[h] Those born only once, with physical birth[i], will never receive this gift. But now I have told you how to get this true spiritual life. [64]But some of you don't believe me." (For Jesus knew from the beginning who didn't believe and knew the one who would betray him.)

[65]And he remarked, "That is what I meant when I said that no one can come to me unless the Father attracts him to me."

[66]At this point many of his disciples turned away and deserted him.

[67]Then Jesus turned to the Twelve and asked, "Are you going too?"

[68]Simon Peter replied, "Master, to whom shall we go? You alone have the words that give eternal life, [69]and we believe them and know you are the holy Son of God."

---

f. Implied. Literally, "Son of Man."   g. Literally, "the Son of Man."   h. Literally, "It is the Spirit who quickens."   i. See Jn 1:13. Literally, "the flesh profits nothing."

⁷⁰**Then Jesus said,** "I chose the twelve of you, and one is a devil. ⁷¹**He was speaking of Judas, son of Simon Iscariot, one of the Twelve, who would betray him.**

9.

THE APOSTOLIC SCHOOL

Jesus Works a Miracle in Jerusalem
Jn 5:1–17

¹Afterwards Jesus returned to Jerusalem for one of the Jewish religious holidays. ²Inside the city, near the Sheep Gate, was Bethesda Pool, with five covered platforms or porches surrounding it. ³Crowds of sick folks—lame, blind, or with paralyzed limbs—lay on the platforms (waiting for a certain movement of the water, ⁴for an angel of the Lord came from time to time and disturbed the water, and the first person to step down into it afterwards was healed).ª

⁵One of the men lying there had been sick for thirty-eight years. ⁶When Jesus saw him and knew how long he had been ill, he asked him, "Would you like to get well?"

⁷"I can't," the sick man said, "for I have no one to help me into the pool at the movement of the water. While I am trying to get there, someone else always gets in ahead of me."

⁸Jesus told him, "Stand up, roll up your sleeping mat and go on home!"

⁹Instantly, the man was healed! He rolled up the mat and began walking!

But it was on the Sabbath when this miracle was

The feast is Passover. Archaeologists have found the ruins of this pool a little north of the Temple. Some think the pool was fed by springs which bubbled up at intervals.

---

a. Many of the ancient manuscripts omit the material within the parentheses.

done. ¹⁰So the Jewish leaders objected. They said to the man who was cured, "You can't work on the Sabbath! It's illegal to carry that sleeping mat!"

¹¹"The man who healed me told me to," was his reply.

¹²"Who said such a thing as that?" they demanded.

¹³The man didn't know, and Jesus had disappeared into the crowd. ¹⁴But afterwards Jesus found him in the Temple and told him, "Now you are well; don't sin as you did before,[b] or something even worse may happen to you."

¹⁵Then the man went to find the Jewish leaders and told them it was Jesus who had healed him.

¹⁶So they began harassing Jesus as a Sabbath breaker. ¹⁷But Jesus replied, "My Father constantly does good,[c] and I'm following his example."

The Role of the Son
Jn 5:18–47

¹⁸Then the Jewish leaders were all the more eager to kill him because in addition to disobeying their Sabbath laws, he had spoken of God as his Father, thereby making himself equal with God.

¹⁹Jesus replied, "The Son can do nothing by himself. He does only what he sees the Father doing, and in the same way. ²⁰For the Father loves the Son, and tells him everything he is doing; and the Son will do far more awesome miracles than this man's healing. ²¹He will even raise from the dead anyone he wants to, just as the Father does. ²²And the Father leaves all judgment of sin to his Son, ²³so that everyone will honor the Son, just as they honor the Father. But if you refuse to honor God's Son, whom he sent to you, then you are

---

b. Implied. Literally, "sin no more."   c. Implied. Literally, "My Father works even until now, and I work."

certainly not honoring the Father.

²⁴"I say emphatically that anyone who listens to my message and believes in God who sent me has eternal life, and will never be damned for his sins, but has already passed out of death into life. ²⁵And I solemnly declare that the time is coming, in fact, it is here, when the dead shall hear my voice—the voice of the Son of God—and those who listen shall live. ²⁶The Father has life in himself, and has granted his Son to have life in himself, ²⁷and to judge the sins of all mankind because he is the Son of Man. ²⁸Don't be surprised! Indeed the time is coming when all the dead in their graves shall hear the voice of God's Son, ²⁹and shall rise again—those who have done good, to eternal life; and those who have continued in evil, to judgment.

³⁰"But I pass no judgment without consulting the Father. I judge as I am told. And my judgment is absolutely fair and just, for it is according to the will of God who sent me and is not merely my own.

³¹"When I make claims about myself they aren't believed, ³²,³³but someone else, yes, John the Baptist,[d] is making these claims for me too. You have gone out to listen to his preaching, and I can assure you that all he says about me is true! ³⁴But the truest witness I have is not from a man, though I have reminded you about John's witness so that you will believe in men and be saved. ³⁵John shone brightly for a while, and you benefited and rejoiced, ³⁶but I have a greater witness than John. I refer to the miracles I do; these have been assigned me by the Father, and they prove that the Father has sent me. ³⁷And the Father himself has also testified about me, though not appearing to you personally, or speaking to you directly. ³⁸But you

---

d. Implied. However, most commentators believe the reference is to the witness of his Father. See verse 37.

are not listening to him, for you refuse to believe me—the one sent to you with God's message.

³⁹"You search the Scriptures, for you believe they give you eternal life. And the Scriptures point to me! ⁴⁰Yet you won't come to me so that I can give you this life eternal!

⁴¹,⁴²"Your approval or disapproval means nothing to me, for as I know so well, you don't have God's love within you. ⁴³I know, because I have come to you representing my Father and you refuse to welcome me, though you readily enough receive those who aren't sent from him, but represent only themselves! ⁴⁴No wonder you can't believe! For you gladly honor each other, but you don't care about the honor that comes from the only God!

⁴⁵"Yet it is not I who will accuse you of this to the Father—Moses will! Moses, on whose laws you set your hopes of heaven. ⁴⁶For you have refused to believe Moses. He wrote about me, but you refuse to believe him, so you refuse to believe in me. ⁴⁷And since you don't believe what he wrote, no wonder you don't believe me either."

Ritual or Intention
Mk 7:1–16, Mt 15:12–20)

¹One day some Jewish religious leaders arrived from Jerusalem to investigate him, ²and noticed that some of his disciples failed to follow the usual Jewish rituals before eating. ³(For the Jews, especially the Pharisees, will never eat until they have sprinkled their arms to the elbows,[a] as required by their ancient traditions. ⁴So when they come home from the market they must always

a. Literally, "to wash with the fist."

sprinkle themselves in this way before touching any food. This is but one of many examples of laws and regulations they have clung to for centuries, and still follow, such as their ceremony of cleansing for pots, pans and dishes.)

⁵So the religious leaders asked him, "Why don't your disciples follow our age-old customs? For they eat without first performing the washing ceremony."

⁶,⁷Jesus replied, "You bunch of hypocrites! Isaiah the prophet described you very well when he said, 'These people speak very prettily about the Lord but they have no love for him at all. Their worship is a farce, for they claim that God commands the people to obey their petty rules.' How right Isaiah was! ⁸For you ignore God's specific orders and substitute your own traditions. ⁹You are simply rejecting God's laws and trampling them under your feet for the sake of tradition.

¹⁰"For instance, Moses gave you this law from God: 'Honor your father and mother.' And he said that anyone who speaks against his father or mother must die. ¹¹But you say it is perfectly all right for a man to disregard his needy parents, telling them, 'Sorry, I can't help you! For I have given to God what I could have given to you.' ¹²,¹³And so you break the law of God in order to protect your man-made tradition. And this is only one example. There are many, many others."

¹⁴Then Jesus called to the crowd to come and hear. "All of you listen," he said, "and try to understand. ¹⁵,¹⁶ᵇYour souls aren't harmed by what you eat, but by what you think and say!"ᶜ

¹²Then the disciples came and told him, "You offended the Pharisees by that remark."

¹³,¹⁴Jesus replied, "Every plant not planted by my Father shall be rooted up, so ignore them.

---

b. Verse 16 is omitted in many of the ancient manuscripts. "If any man has ears to hear, let him hear."
c. Literally, "what proceeds out of the man defiles the man."

They are blind guides leading the blind, and both will fall into a ditch."

¹⁵Then Peter asked Jesus to explain what he meant when he said that people are not defiled by non-kosher food.

¹⁶"Don't you understand?" Jesus asked him. ¹⁷"Don't you see that anything you eat passes through the digestive tract and out again? ¹⁸But evil words come from an evil heart, and defile the man who says them. ¹⁹For from the heart come evil thoughts, murder, adultery, fornication, theft, lying and slander. ²⁰These are what defile; but there is no spiritual defilement from eating without first going through the ritual of ceremonial handwashing!"

The Death of John the Baptist
Mk 6:14–29

¹⁴King Herod soon heard about Jesus, for his miracles were talked about everywhere. The king thought Jesus was John the Baptist come back to life again. So the people were saying, "No wonder he can do such miracles." ¹⁵Others thought Jesus was Elijah the ancient prophet, now returned to life again; still others claimed he was a new prophet like the great ones of the past.

¹⁶"No," Herod said, "it is John, the man I beheaded. He has come back from the dead."

¹⁷,¹⁸For Herod had sent soldiers to arrest and imprison John because he kept saying it was wrong for the king to marry Herodias, his brother Philip's wife. ¹⁹Herodias wanted John killed in revenge, but without Herod's approval she was powerless. ²⁰And Herod respected John, knowing that he was a good and holy man, and so he

This incident took place at Machaerus on the eastern shore of the Dead Sea where Herod had a fortress and a palace.

kept him under his protection. Herod was disturbed whenever he talked with John, but even so he liked to listen to him.

²¹Herodias' chance finally came. It was Herod's birthday and he gave a stag party for his palace aides, army officers, and the leading citizens of Galilee. ²²,²³Then Herodias' daughter came in and danced before them and greatly pleased them all.

"Ask me for anything you like," the king vowed, "even half of my kingdom, and I will give it to you!"

²⁴She went out and consulted her mother, who told her, "Ask for John the Baptist's head!"

²⁵So she hurried back to the king and told him, "I want the head of John the Baptist—right now—on a tray!"

²⁶Then the king was sorry, but he was embarrassed to break his oath in front of his guests. ²⁷So he sent one of his bodyguards to the prison to cut off John's head and bring it to him. The soldier killed John in the prison, ²⁸and brought back his head on a tray, and gave it to the girl and she took it to her mother.

²⁹When John's disciples heard what had happened, they came for his body and buried it.

Second Miracle of the Loaves
Mk 8:1-9

¹,²One day about this time as another great crowd gathered, the people ran out of food again. Jesus called his disciples to discuss the situation.

"I pity these people," he said, "for they have been here three days, and have nothing left to eat. ³And if I send them home without feeding them, they will faint along the road! For some of them have come a long distance."

⁴"Are we supposed to find food for them here in the desert?" his disciples scoffed.

⁵"How many loaves of bread do you have?" he asked.

"Seven," they replied. ⁶So he told the crowd to sit down on the ground. Then he took the seven loaves, thanked God for them, broke them into pieces and passed them to his disciples; and the disciples placed them before the people. ⁷A few small fish were found, too, so Jesus also blessed these and told the disciples to serve them.

⁸,⁹And the whole crowd ate until they were full, and afterwards he sent them home. There were about 4,000 people in the crowd that day and when the scraps were picked up after the meal, there were seven very large basketfuls left over!

Jewish Leaders Seek a Sign
Mk 8:10–12

¹⁰Immediately after this he got into a boat with his disciples and came to the region of Dalmanutha. ¹¹When the local Jewish leaders learned of his arrival they came to argue with him.

The site of Dalmanutha has not been identified.

"Do a miracle for us," they said. "Make something happen in the sky. Then we will believe in you."ᵃ

¹²He sighed deeply when he heard this and he said, "Certainly not. How many more miracles do you people need?"ᵇ

Jesus Is the Sign
Lk 11:29–36

²⁹,³⁰As the crowd pressed in upon him, he

---

a. Literally, "to test him."   b. Literally, "Why does this generation seek a sign?"

preached them this sermon: "These are evil times, with evil people. They keep asking for some strange happening in the skies [to prove I am the Messiah^c], but the only proof I will give them is a miracle like that of Jonah, whose experiences proved to the people of Nineveh that God had sent him. My similar experience will prove that God has sent me to these people.

31"And at the Judgment Day the Queen of Sheba^h shall arise and point her finger at this generation, condemning it, for she went on a long, hard journey to listen to the wisdom of Solomon; but one far greater than Solomon is here [and few pay any attention^c].

32"The men of Nineveh, too, shall arise and condemn this nation, for they repented at the teaching of Jonah; and someone far greater than Jonah is here (but this nation won't listen^c). 33 No one lights a lamp and hides it! Instead, he puts it on a lampstand to give light to all who enter the room. 34Your eyes light up your inward being. A pure eye lets sunshine into your soul. A lustful eye shuts out the light and plunges you into darkness. 35So watch out that the sunshine isn't blotted out. 36If you are filled with light within, with no dark corners, then your face will be radiant too, as though a floodlight is beamed upon you."

Jonah went from Jewish Palestine to Assyrian Nineveh to preach and these Gentiles believed his message.

Jesus Warns Against Worldliness
Mk 8:13–21

13So he got back into the boat and left them, and crossed to the other side of the lake. 14But the disciples had forgotten to stock up on food before they left, and had only one loaf of bread in the boat.

15As they were crossing, Jesus said to them very

---

c. Implied.   h. Literally, "Queen of the South." See 1 Kgs, chapter 10.

solemnly, "Beware of the yeast of King Herod and of the Pharisees."

¹⁶"What does he mean?" the disciples asked each other. They finally decided that he must be talking about their forgetting to bring bread.

¹⁷Jesus realized what they were discussing and said, "No, that isn't it at all! Can't you understand? Are your hearts too hard to take it in? ¹⁸'Your eyes are to see with—why don't you look? Why don't you open your ears and listen?' Don't you remember anything at all?

¹⁹"What about the 5,000 men I fed with five loaves of bread? How many basketfuls of scraps did you pick up afterwards?"

"Twelve," they said.

²⁰"And when I fed the 4,000 with seven loaves, how much was left?"

"Seven basketfuls," they said.

²¹"And yet you think I'm worried that we have no bread?"ᶜ

Cure of the Blind Man
Mk 8:22–26

²²When they arrived at Bethsaida, some people brought a blind man to him and begged him to touch and heal him. ²³Jesus took the blind man by the hand and led him out of the village, and spat upon his eyes, and laid his hands over them.

"Can you see anything now?" Jesus asked him.

²⁴The man looked around. "Yes!" he said, "I see men! But I can't see them very clearly; they look like tree trunks walking around!"

²⁵Then Jesus placed his hands over the man's eyes again and as the man stared intently, his sight was completely restored, and he saw every-

---

c. Literally, "Do you not yet understand?"

thing clearly, drinking in the sights around him.

²⁶Jesus sent him home to his family. "Don't even go back to the village first," he said.

Peter Recognizes Christ
Mt 16:13–20

¹³When Jesus came to Caesarea Philippi, he asked his disciples, "Who are the people saying Iᵇ am?"

¹⁴"Well," they replied, "some say John the Baptist; some, Elijah; some, Jeremiah or one of the other prophets."

¹⁵Then he asked them, "Who do *you* think I am?"

¹⁶Simon Peter answered, "The Christ, the Messiah, the Son of the living God."

¹⁷"God has blessed you, Simon, son of Jonah," Jesus said, "for my Father in heaven has personally revealed this to you—this is not from any human source. ¹⁸You are Peter, a stone; and upon this rock I will build my church; and all the powers of hell shall not prevail against it. ¹⁹And I will give you the keys of the Kingdom of Heaven; whatever doors you lock on earth shall be locked in heaven; and whatever doors you open on earth shall be open in heaven!"

²⁰Then he warned the disciples against telling others that he was the Messiah.

Caesarea Philippi lay in the foothills of Mount Hermon, north of Galilee. It was a place to escape the summer heat. It had been rebuilt by the tetrarch Philip and named after Caesar Augustus.

Jesus Predicts His Death
Mk 8:31–9:1

³¹Then he began to tell them about the terrible things heᵈ would suffer, and that he would be rejected by the elders, and the Chief Priests and the other Jewish leaders—and be killed, and that he

b. Literally, "the Son of Man."

d. Literally, "the Son of Man."

would rise again three days afterwards. [32]He talked about it quite frankly with them, so Peter took him aside and chided him.[e] "You shouldn't say things like that," he told Jesus.

[33]Jesus turned and looked at his disciples and then said to Peter very sternly, "Satan, get behind me! You are looking at this only from a human point of view and not from God's."

[34]Then he called his disciples and the crowds to come over and listen. "If any of you wants to be my follower," he told them, "you must put aside your own pleasures and shoulder your cross, and follow me closely. [35]If you insist on saving your life, you will lose it. Only those who throw away their lives for my sake and for the sake of the Good News will ever know what it means to really live.

[36]"And how does a man benefit if he gains the whole world and loses his soul in the process? [37]For is anything worth more than his soul? [38]And anyone who is ashamed of me and my message in these days of unbelief and sin, I, the Messiah,[d] will be ashamed of him when I return in the glory of my Father, with the holy angels."

[1]Jesus went on to say to his disciples, "Some of you who are standing here right now will live to see the Kingdom of God arrive in great power!"

The Transfiguration
Mt 17:1-13

[1]Six days later Jesus took Peter, James, and his brother John to the top of a high and lonely hill, [2]and as they watched, his appearance changed so that his face shone like the sun and his clothing became dazzling white.

[3]Suddenly Moses and Elijah appeared and were

The site is unknown. An old tradition names Mount Tabor but excavations have shown a fortress here which makes it unlikely. Mount Hermon is suggested because Jesus was in the area.

e. Literally, "Peter began to rebuke him." d. Literally, "the Son of Man."

talking with him. [4]Peter blurted out, "Sir, it's wonderful that we can be here! If you want me to, I'll make three shelters,[a] one for you and one for Moses and one for Elijah."

[5]But even as he said it, a bright cloud came over them, and a voice from the cloud said, "*This* is my beloved Son, and I am wonderfully pleased with him. Obey[b] *him*."

[6]At this the disciples fell face downward to the ground, terribly frightened. [7]Jesus came over and touched them. "Get up," he said, "don't be afraid."

[8]And when they looked, only Jesus was with them.

[9]As they were going down the mountain, Jesus commanded them not to tell anyone what they had seen until after he had risen from the dead.

[10]His disciples asked, "Why do the Jewish leaders insist Elijah must return before the Messiah comes?"[c]

[11]Jesus replied, "They are right. Elijah must come and set everything in order. [12]And, in fact, he has already come, but he wasn't recognized, and was badly mistreated by many. And I, the Messiah[d], shall also suffer at their hands."

[13]Then the disciples realized he was speaking of John the Baptist.

Cure of the Epileptic Boy
Mk 9:14–29

[14]At the bottom of the mountain they found a great crowd surrounding the other nine disciples, as some Jewish leaders argued with them. [15]The crowd watched Jesus in awe as he came toward them, and then ran to greet him. [16]"What's all the argument about?" he asked.

Ancient writers suggest Moses and Elijah represent the Law and the Prophets testifying to Christ, the fulfillment of the Old Law and initiator of the New.

---

a. Literally, "three tabernacles" or "tents." What was in Peter's mind is not explained.   b. Literally, "hear him."   c. Implied. Literally, "that Elijah must come first."   d. Literally, "the Son of Man."

¹⁷One of the men in the crowd spoke up and said, "Teacher, I brought my son for you to heal—he can't talk because he is possessed by a demon. ¹⁸And whenever the demon is in control of him it dashes him to the ground and makes him foam at the mouth and grind his teeth and become rigid.ᶜ So I begged your disciples to cast out the demon, but they couldn't do it."

¹⁹Jesus said [to his disciplesᵇ], "Oh, what tiny faith you have;ᵈ how much longer must I be with you until you believe? How much longer must I be patient with you? Bring the boy to me."

²⁰So they brought the boy, but when he saw Jesus the demon convulsed the child horribly, and he fell to the ground writhing and foaming at the mouth.

²¹"How long has he been this way?" Jesus asked the father.

And he replied, "Since he was very small, ²²and the demon often makes him fall into the fire or into water to kill him. Oh, have mercy on us and do something if you can."

²³"If I can?" Jesus asked. "*Anything* is possible if you have faith."

²⁴The father instantly replied, "I *do* have faith; oh, help me to have *more*!"

²⁵When Jesus saw the crowd was growing he rebuked the demon.

"O demon of deafness and dumbness," he said, "I command you to come out of this child and enter him no more!"

²⁶Then the demon screamed terribly and convulsed the boy again and left him; and the boy lay there limp and motionless, to all appearance dead. A murmur ran through the crowd—"He is dead." ²⁷But Jesus took him by the hand and helped him to his feet and he stood up and was all

b. Implied.   c. Or, "is growing weaker day by day."   d. Literally, "O unbelieving generation."

right! [28]Afterwards, when Jesus was alone in the house with his disciples, they asked him, "Why couldn't we cast that demon out?"

[29]Jesus replied, "Cases like this require prayer."[e]

Another Prediction of Death
Mk 9:30–32

[30,31]Leaving that region they traveled through Galilee where he tried to avoid all publicity in order to spend more time with his disciples, teaching them. He would say to them, "I, the Messiah,[a] am going to be betrayed and killed and three days later I will return to life again."

[32]But they didn't understand and were afraid to ask him what he meant.

The Temple Tax
Mt 17:24–27

[24]On their arrival in Capernaum, the Temple tax collectors came to Peter and asked him, "Doesn't your master pay taxes?"

[25]"Of course he does," Peter replied.

Then he went into the house to talk to Jesus about it, but before he had a chance to speak, Jesus asked him, "What do you think, Peter? Do kings levy assessments against their own people, or against conquered foreigners?"

[26,27]"Against the foreigners," Peter replied.

"Well, then," Jesus said, "the citizens are free! However, we don't want to offend them, so go down to the shore and throw in a line, and open the mouth of the first fish you catch. You will find a coin to cover the taxes for both of us; take it and pay them."

Every male Jew, twenty and over had to pay a two-drachma tax for the upkeep of the Temple. This was two day's wages for the ordinary man.

e. "And fasting" is added in some manuscripts, but not the most ancient.

a. Literally, "the Son of Man."

Be as a Child
Mk 9:33–34, Mt 18:2–22

³³And so they arrived in Capernaum. When they were settled in the house where they were to stay he asked them, "What were you discussing out on the road?"

³⁴But they were ashamed to answer, for they had been arguing about which of them was the greatest!

²Jesus called a small child over to him and set the little fellow down among them, ³and said, "Unless you turn to God from your sins and become as little children, you will never get into the Kingdom of Heaven. ⁴Therefore anyone who humbles himself as this little child, is the greatest in the Kingdom of Heaven. ⁵And any of you who welcomes a little child like this because you are mine, is welcoming me and caring for me. ⁶But if any of you causes one of these little ones who trusts in me to lose his faith,ᵃ it would be better for you to have a rock tied to your neck and be thrown into the sea.

⁷"Woe upon the world for all its evils.ᵇ Temptation to do wrong is inevitable, but woe to the man who does the tempting. ⁸So if your hand or foot causes you to sin, cut it off and throw it away. Better to enter heaven crippled than to be in hell with both of your hands and feet. ⁹And if your eye causes you to sin, gouge it out and throw it away. Better to enter heaven with one eye than to be in hell with two.

¹⁰"Beware that you don't look down upon a single one of these little children. For I tell you that in heaven their angels have constant accessᶜ to my Father. ¹¹And I, the Messiah,ᵈ came to save the lost.ᵉ

---

a. Literally, "cause to stumble." b. Literally, "because of occasions of stumbling." c. "Do always behold . . ." d. Literally, "the Son of Man." e. This verse is omitted in many manuscripts, some ancient.

¹²"If a man has a hundred sheep, and one wanders away and is lost, what will he do? Won't he leave the ninety-nine others and go out into the hills to search for the lost one? ¹³And if he finds it, he will rejoice over it more than over the ninety-nine others safe at home! ¹⁴Just so, it is not my Father's will that even one of these little ones should perish.

¹⁵"If a brother sins against you, go to him privately and confront him with his fault. If he listens and confesses it, you have won back a brother. ¹⁶But if not, then take one or two others with you and go back to him again, proving everything you say by these witnesses. ¹⁷If he still refuses to listen, then take your case to the church, and if the church's verdict favors you, but he won't accept it, then the church should excommunicate him.ᶠ ¹⁸And I tell you this—whatever you bind on earth is bound in heaven, and whatever you free on earth will be freed in heaven.

¹⁹"I also tell you this—if two of you agree down here on earth concerning anything you ask for, my Father in heaven will do it for you. ²⁰For where two or three gather together because they are mine, I will be right there among them."

²¹Then Peter came to him and asked, "Sir, how often should I forgive a brother who sins against me? Seven times?"

²²"No!" Jesus replied, "seventy times seven!"

The Power of Jesus' Name
Mk 9:38–50

³⁸One of his disciples, John, told him one day, "Teacher, we saw a man using your name to cast out demons; but we told him not to, for he isn't one of our group."

---

f. Literally, "let him be to you as the Gentile and the publican."

[39]"Don't forbid him!" **Jesus said.** "For no one doing miracles in my name will quickly turn against me.[f][40]Anyone who isn't against us is for us. [41]If anyone so much as gives you a cup of water because you are Christ's—I say this solemnly—he won't lose his reward. [42]But if someone causes one of these little ones who believe in me to lose faith—it would be better for that man if a huge millstone were tied around his neck and he were thrown into the sea.

[43,44g]"If your hand does wrong, cut it off. Better live forever with one hand than be thrown into the unquenchable fires of hell with two! [45,46g]If your foot carries you toward evil, cut it off! Better be lame and live forever than have two feet that carry you to hell.

[47]"And if your eye is sinful, gouge it out. Better enter the Kingdom of God half blind than have two eyes and see the fires of hell, [48]where the worm never dies, and the fire never goes out—[49]where all are salted with fire.[h]

[50]"Good salt is worthless if it loses its saltiness; it can't season anything. So don't lose your flavor! Live in peace with each other."

f. Literally, "will be able to speak evil of me." g. Verses 44 and 46 (which are identical with verse 48) are omitted in some of the ancient manuscripts. h. Literally, "For everyone shall be salted with fire."

10.

THE JUDEAN MINISTRY

The Samaritan Rejection
Lk 9:51–58

[51]As the time drew near for his return to heaven, he moved steadily onward towards Jerusalem with an iron will.

[52]One day he sent messengers ahead to reserve rooms for them in a Samaritan village. [53]But they were turned away! The people of the village refused to have anything to do with them because they were headed for Jerusalem.[g]

[54]When word came back of what had happened, James and John said to Jesus, "Master, shall we order fire down from heaven to burn them up?" [55]But Jesus turned and rebuked them,[h] [56]and they went on to another village.

John and James live up to the name Jesus gave them, "Sons of Thunder." They expected Jesus to act like Elijah. (2 Kgs 1:10–12).

[57]As they were walking along someone said to Jesus, "I will always follow you no matter where you go."

[58]But Jesus replied, "Remember, I don't even own a place to lay my head. Foxes have dens to live in, and birds have nests, but I, the Messiah,[i] have no earthly home at all."

---

g. A typical case of discrimination (cf. Jn 4:9). The Jews called the Samaritans "half-breeds," so the Samaritans naturally hated the Jews. h. Later manuscripts add to verses 55 and 56, "And Jesus said, 'You don't realize what your hearts are like. For the Son of Man has not come to destroy men's lives, but to save them." i. Literally, "the Son of Man."

The Delaying Disciples
Lk 9:59–62

⁵⁹Another time, when he invited a man to come with him and to be his disciple, the man agreed— but wanted to wait until his father's death.ʲ

⁶⁰Jesus replied, "Let those without eternal life concern themselves with things like that.ᵏ Your duty is to come and preach the coming of the Kingdom of God to all the world."

Jesus demands more than did the prophet Elisha. See 1 Kgs 19:19–21.

⁶¹Another said, "Yes, Lord, I will come, but first let me ask permission of those at home."ˡ

⁶²But Jesus told him, "Anyone who lets himself be distracted from the work I plan for him is not fit for the Kingdom of God."

Seventy Disciples Sent Out
Lk 10:1–12, Mt 11:21–24, Lk 10:16

¹The Lord now chose seventy other disciples and sent them on ahead in pairs to all the towns and villages he planned to visit later.

²These were his instructions to them: "Plead with the Lord of the harvest to send out more laborers to help you, for the harvest is so plentiful and the workers so few. ³Go now, and remember that I am sending you out as lambs among wolves. ⁴Don't take any money with you, or a beggar's bag, or even an extra pair of shoes. And don't waste time along the way.ᵃ

⁵"Whenever you enter a home, give it your blessing. ⁶If it is worthy of the blessing, the blessing will stand; if not, the blessing will return to you.

⁷"When you enter a village, don't shift around from home to home, but stay in one place, eating and drinking without question whatever is set be-

---

j. Literally, "But he said, 'Lord, suffer me first to go and bury my father,' "—perhaps meaning that the man could, when his father died, collect the inheritance and have some security.   k. Or, "Let those who are spiritually dead care for their own dead."   l. Literally, "bid them farewell at home."

a. Literally, "Salute no one in the way."

fore you. And don't hesitate to accept hospitality, for the workman is worthy of his wages!

[8,9]"If a town welcomes you, follow these two rules: (1) Eat whatever is set before you. (2) Heal the sick; and as you heal them, say, 'The Kingdom of God is very near you now.'

[10]"But if a town refuses you, go out into its streets and say, [11]'We wipe the dust of your town from our feet as a public announcement of your doom. Never forget how close you were to the Kingdom of God!' [12]Even wicked Sodom will be better off than such a city on the Judgment Day.

[21]"Woe to you, Chorazin, and woe to you, Bethsaida! For if the miracles I did in your streets had been done in wicked Tyre and Sidon[h] their people would have repented long ago in shame and humility. [22]Truly Tyre and Sidon will be better off on the Judgment Day than you! [23]And Capernaum, though highly honored,[i] shall go down to hell! For if the marvelous miracles I did in you had been done in Sodom,[h] it would still be here today. [24]Truly, Sodom will be better off at the Judgment Day than you."

[16]Then he said to the disciples, "Those who welcome you are welcoming me. And those who reject you are rejecting me. And those who reject me are rejecting God who sent me."

Chorazin, the present Kerazeh, lay a few miles north of Capernaum. The Gospels do not mention what Jesus did there.

Return of the Seventy
Lk 10:17–24, Mt 11:25–30

[17]When the seventy disciples returned, they joyfully reported to him, "Even the demons obey us when we use your name."

[18]"Yes," he told them, "I saw Satan falling from

---

h. Cities destroyed by God in judgment for their wickedness. For a description of this event, see Ez, chapters 26-28. i. Highly honored by Christ's being there.

heaven as a flash of lightning! ¹⁹And I have given you authority over all the power of the Enemy, and to walk among serpents and scorpions and to crush them. Nothing shall injure you! ²⁰However, the important thing is not that demons obey you, but that your names are registered as citizens of heaven."

²¹Then he was filled with the joy of the Holy Spirit and said, "I praise you, O Father, Lord of heaven and earth, for hiding these things from the intellectuals and worldly wise and for revealing them to those who are as trusting as little children.ᶜ Yes, thank you, Father, for that is the way you wanted it. ²²I am the Agent of my Father in everything; and no one really knows the Son except the Father, and no one really knows the Father except the Son and those to whom the Son chooses to reveal him."

²³Then, turning to the twelve disciples, he said quietly, "How privileged you are to see what you have seen. ²⁴Many a prophet and king of old has longed for these days, to see and hear what you have seen and heard!"

²⁵And Jesus prayed this prayer: "O Father, Lord of heaven and earth, thank you for hiding the truth from those who think themselves so wise, and for revealing it to little children. ²⁶Yes, Father, for it pleased you to do it this way! . . .

²⁷"Everything has been entrusted to me by my Father. Only the Father knows the Son, and the Father is known only by the Son and by those to whom the Son reveals him. ²⁸Come to me and I will give you rest—all of you who work so hard beneath a heavy yoke. ²⁹,³⁰Wear my yoke—for it fits perfectly—and let me teach you; for I am gentle and humble, and you shall find rest for your souls; for I give you only light burdens."

c. Literally, "babies."

The Our Father
Lk 11:1–2, Mt 6:9–15

¹Once when Jesus had been out praying, one of his disciples came to him as he finished and said, "Lord, teach us a prayer to recite[a] just as John taught one to his disciples."

⁹"Our Father in heaven, we honor your holy name. ¹⁰We ask that your kingdom will come now. May your will be done here on earth, just as it is in heaven. ¹¹Give us our food again today, as usual, ¹²and forgive us our sins, just as we have forgiven those who have sinned against us. ¹³Don't bring us into temptation, but deliver us from the Evil One.[a] Amen. ¹⁴,¹⁵Your heavenly Father will forgive you if you forgive those who sin against you; but if *you* refuse to forgive *them, he* will not forgive *you*."

Matthew's version has seven petitions; Luke's six.

Jesus Visits Martha and Mary
Lk 10:38–42

³⁸As Jesus and the disciples continued on their way to Jerusalem[i] they came to a village where a woman named Martha welcomed them into her home. ³⁹Her sister Mary sat on the floor, listening to Jesus as he talked.

⁴⁰But Martha was the jittery type, and was worrying over the big dinner she was preparing.

She came to Jesus and said, "Sir, doesn't it seem unfair to you that my sister just sits here while I do all the work? Tell her to come and help me."

⁴¹But the Lord said to her, "Martha, dear friend,[j] you are so upset over all these details! ⁴²There is really only one thing worth being concerned about. Mary has discovered it—and I won't take it away from her!"

John 11:1 tells that the village is Bethany, a town on the east side of the Mount of Olives.

a. Implied.

a. Or, "from evil." Some manuscripts add here, "For yours is the kingdom and the power and the glory forever. Amen."

i. Implied.   j. Literally, "Martha, Martha."

The Disbelieving Jews
Jn 12:37–47

37But despite all the miracles he had done, most of the people would not believe he was the Messiah. 38This is exactly what Isaiah the prophet had predicted: "Lord, who will believe us? Who will accept God's mighty miracles as proof?"f 39But they couldn't believe, for as Isaiah also said: 40"Godg has blinded their eyes and hardened their hearts so that they can neither see nor understand nor turn to me to heal them." 41Isaiah was referring to Jesus when he made this prediction, for he had seen a vision of the Messiah's glory.

42However, even many of the Jewish leaders believed him to be the Messiah but wouldn't admit it to anyone because of their fear that the Pharisees would excommunicate them from the synagogue; 43for they loved the praise of men more than the praise of God.

44Jesus shouted to the crowds, "If you trust me, you are really trusting God. 45For when you see me, you are seeing the one who sent me. 46I have come as a Light to shine in this dark world, so that all who put their trust in me will no longer wander in the darkness. 47If anyone hears me and doesn't obey me, I am not his judge—for I have come to save the world and not to judge it."

The Feast of Tabernacles
Jn 7:1–9

1After this, Jesus went to Galilee, going from village to village, for he wanted to stay out of Judea where the Jewish leaders were plotting his death. 2But soon it was time for the Tabernacle Cere-

---

f. Literally, "To whom has the arm of the Lord been revealed?" Is 53:1.   g. Literally, "He." The Greek here is a very free rendering, or paraphrase, of Is 6:10.

monies, one of the annual Jewish holidays, [3]and Jesus' brothers urged him to go to Judea for the celebration.

"Go where more people can see your miracles!" they scoffed. [4]"You can't be famous when you hide like this! If you're so great, prove it to the world!" [5]For even his brothers didn't believe in him.

[6]Jesus replied, "It is not the right time for me to go now. But you can go anytime and it will make no difference, [7]for the world can't hate you; but it does hate me, because I accuse it of sin and evil. [8]You go on, and I'll come later[a] when it is the right time." [9]So he remained in Galilee.

Jesus had once remarked that a prophet is without honor in his own country and we might add here "and in his own family."

Jesus Appears in the Temple
Jn 7:10–24

[10]But after his brothers had left for the celebration, then he went too, though secretly, staying out of the public eye. [11]The Jewish leaders tried to find him at the celebration and kept asking if anyone had seen him. [12]There was a lot of discussion about him among the crowds. Some said, "He's a wonderful man," while others said, "No, he's duping the public." [13]But no one had the courage to speak out for him in public for fear of reprisals from the Jewish leaders.

[14]Then, midway through the festival, Jesus went up to the Temple and preached openly. [15]The Jewish leaders were surprised when they heard him. "How can he know so much when he's never been to our schools?" they asked.

[16]So Jesus told them, "I'm not teaching you my own thoughts, but those of God who sent me. [17]If any of you really determines to do God's will,

---

a. Literally, "I go not up (yet) unto this feast." The word "yet" is included in the text of many ancient manuscripts.

then you will certainly know whether my teaching is from God or is merely my own. [18]Anyone presenting his own ideas is looking for praise for himself, but anyone seeking to honor the one who sent him is a good and true person. [19]None of *you* obeys the laws of Moses! So why pick on *me* for breaking them? Why kill *me* for this?"

[20]The crowd replied, "You're out of your mind! Who's trying to kill you?"

[21,22,23]Jesus replied, "I worked on the Sabbath by healing a man, and you were surprised. But you work on the Sabbath, too, whenever you obey Moses' law of circumcision (actually, however, this tradition of circumcision is older than the Mosaic law); for if the correct time for circumcising your children falls on the Sabbath, you go ahead and do it, as you should. So why should I be condemned for making a man completely well on the Sabbath? [24]Think this through and you will see that I am right."

Jesus Defends His Mission
Jn 7:25–31

[25]Some of the people who lived there in Jerusalem said among themselves, "Isn't this the man they are trying to kill? [26]But here he is preaching in public, and they say nothing to him. Can it be that our leaders have learned, after all, that he really is the Messiah? [27]But how could he be? For we know where this man was born; when Christ comes, he will just appear and no one will know where he comes from."

[28]So Jesus, in a sermon in the Temple, called out, "Yes, you know me and where I was born and raised, but I am the representative of one you

don't know, and he is Truth. ²⁹I know him because I was with him, and he sent me to you."

³⁰Then the Jewish leaders sought to arrest him; but no hand was laid on him, for God's time had not yet come.

³¹Many among the crowds at the Temple believed on him. "After all," they said, "what miracles do you expect the Messiah to do that this man hasn't done?"

Pharisees Try to Arrest Jesus
Jn 7:32–36

³²When the Pharisees heard that the crowds were in this mood, they and the chief priests sent officers to arrest Jesus. ³³But Jesus told them, "[Not yet!ᵇ] I am to be here a little longer. Then I shall return to the one who sent me. ³⁴You will search for me but not find me. And you won't be able to come where I am!"

³⁵The Jewish leaders were puzzled by this statement. "Where is he planning to go?" they asked. "Maybe he is thinking of leaving the country and going as a missionary among the Jews in other lands, or maybe even to the Gentiles! ³⁶What does he mean about our looking for him and not being able to find him, and, 'You won't be able to come where I am'?"

Some Hearers Believe
Jn 7:37–44

³⁷On the last day, the climax of the holidays, Jesus shouted to the crowds, "If anyone is thirsty, let him come to me and drink. ³⁸For the Scriptures

b. Implied.

declare that rivers of living water shall flow from the inmost being of anyone who believes in me."
[39](He was speaking of the Holy Spirit, who would be given to everyone believing in him; but the Spirit had not yet been given, because Jesus had not yet returned to his glory in heaven.)

[40]When the crowds heard him say this, some of them declared, "This man surely is the prophet who will come just before the Messiah." [41,42]Others said, "He *is* the Messiah." Still others, "But he *can't* be! Will the Messiah come from *Galilee*? For the Scriptures clearly state that the Messiah will be born of the royal line of David, in *Bethlehem*, the village where David was born." [43]So the crowd was divided about him. [44]And some wanted him arrested, but no one touched him.

Nicodemus Defends Jesus
Jn 7:45–53

[45]The Temple police who had been sent to arrest him returned to the chief priests and Pharisees. "Why didn't you bring him in?" they demanded.

[46]"He says such wonderful things!" they mumbled. "We've never heard anything like it."

[47]"So you also have been led astray?" the Pharisees mocked. [48]"Is there a single one of us Jewish rulers or Pharisees who believes he is the Messiah? [49]These stupid crowds do, yes; but what do they know about it? A curse upon them anyway!"[c]

[50]Then Nicodemus spoke up. (Remember him? He was the Jewish leader who came secretly to interview Jesus.) [51]"Is it legal to convict a man before he is even tried?" he asked.

[52]They replied, "Are you a wretched Galilean

Nicodemus is still cautious. He does not really defend Jesus but merely argues that the Law be followed.

---

c. Literally, "This multitude is accursed."

too? Search the Scriptures and see for yourself—
no prophets will come from Galilee!" [53d]Then the
meeting broke up and everybody went home.

The Woman Taken in Adultery
Jn 8:1–11

[1]Jesus returned to the Mount of Olives, [2]but early
the next norming he was back again at the Temple. A crowd soon gathered, and he sat down and
talked to them. [3]As he was speaking, the Jewish
leaders and Pharisees brought a woman caught in
adultery and placed her out in front of the staring
crowd.

[4]"Teacher," they said to Jesus, "this woman
was caught in the very act of adultery. [5]Moses' law
says to kill her. What about it?"

[6]They were trying to trap him into saying something they could use against him, but Jesus
stooped down and wrote in the dust with his
finger. [7]They kept demanding an answer, so he
stood up again and said, "All right, hurl the
stones at her until she dies. But only he who never
sinned may throw the first!"

[8]Then he stooped down again and wrote some
more in the dust. [9]And the Jewish leaders slipped
away one by one, beginning with the eldest, until
only Jesus was left in front of the crowd with the
woman.

[10]Then Jesus stood up again and said to her,
"Where are your accusers? Didn't even one of
them condemn you?"

[11]"No, sir," she said.

And Jesus said, "Neither do I. Go and sin no
more."

Some suggest that
Jesus wrote down
the secret sins of the
accusers, others that
He was like a Roman
judge writing down
the charge.

---

d. Most ancient manuscripts omit Jn 7:53–8:11.

Light of the World
Jn 8:12-20

¹²Later, in one of his talks, Jesus said to the people, "I am the Light of the world. So if you follow me, you won't be stumbling through the darkness, for living light will flood your path."

¹³The Pharisees replied, "You are boasting—and lying!"

¹⁴Jesus told them, "These claims are true even though I make them concerning myself. For I know where I came from and where I am going, but you don't know this about me. ¹⁵You pass judgment on me without knowing the facts. I am not judging you now; ¹⁶but if I were, it would be an absolutely correct judgment in every respect, for I have with me the Father who sent me. ¹⁷Your laws say that if two men agree on something that has happened, their witness is accepted as fact. ¹⁸Well, I am one witness, and my Father who sent me is the other."

¹⁹"Where is your father?" they asked.

Jesus answered, "You don't know who I am, so you don't know who my Father is. If you knew me, then you would know him too."

²⁰Jesus made these statements while in the section of the Temple known as the Treasury. But he was not arrested, for his time had not yet run out.

Jesus Predicts His Death
Jn 8:21-59

²¹Later he said to them again, "I am going away; and you will search for me, and die in your sins. And you cannot come where I am going."

²²The Jews asked, "Is he planning suicide?

What does he mean, 'You cannot come where I am going'?"

²³Then he said to them, "You are from below; I am from above. You are of this world; I am not. ²⁴That is why I said that you will die in your sins; for unless you believe that I am the Messiah, the Son of God, you will die in your sins."

²⁵"Tell us who you are," they demanded.

He replied, "I am the one I have always claimed to be. ²⁶I could condemn you for much and teach you much, but I won't, for I say only what I am told to by the one who sent me; and he is Truth." ²⁷But they still didn't understand that he was talking to them about God.ᵃ

²⁸So Jesus said, "When you have killed the Messiah,ᵇ then you will realize that I am he and that I have not been telling you my own ideas, but have spoken what the Father taught me. ²⁹And he who sent me is with me—he has not deserted me—for I always do those things that are pleasing to him."

³⁰,³¹Then many of the Jewish leaders who heard him say these things began believing him to be the Messiah.

Jesus said to them, "You are truly my disciples if you live as I tell you to, ³²and you will know the truth, and the truth will set you free."

³³"But we are descendants of Abraham," they said, "and have never been slaves to any man on earth! What do you mean, 'set free'?"

³⁴Jesus replied, "You are slaves of sin, every one of you. ³⁵And slaves don't have rights, but the Son has every right there is! ³⁶So if the Son sets you free, you will indeed be free— ³⁷(Yes, I realize that you are descendants of Abraham!) And yet some of you are trying to kill me because my message does not find a home within your hearts. ³⁸ I am telling you what I saw when I was with my Father.

a. Literally, "the Father." b. Literally, "when you have lifted up the Son of Man."

But you are following the advice of *your* father."

³⁹"Our father is Abraham," they declared.

"No!" Jesus replied, "for if he were, you would follow his good example. ⁴⁰But instead you are trying to kill me—and all because I told you the truth I heard from God. Abraham wouldn't do a thing like that! ⁴¹No, you are obeying your *real* father when you act that way."

They replied, "We were not born out of wedlock —our true Father is God himself."

⁴²Jesus told them, "If that were so, then you would love me, for I have come to you from God. I am not here on my own, but he sent me. ⁴³Why can't you understand what I am saying? It is because you are prevented from doing so! ⁴⁴For you are the children of your father the devil and you love to do the evil things he does. He was a murderer from the beginning and a hater of truth— there is not an iota of truth in him. When he lies, it is perfectly normal; for he is the father of liars. ⁴⁵And so when I tell the truth, you just naturally don't believe it!

⁴⁶"Which of you can truthfully accuse me of one single sin? [No one!ᶜ] And since I am telling you the truth, why don't you believe me? ⁴⁷Anyone whose Father is God listens gladly to the words of God. Since you don't, it proves you aren't his children."

⁴⁸"You Samaritan! Foreigner! Devil!" the Jewish leaders snarled. "Didn't we say all along you were possessed by a demon?"

⁴⁹"No, Jesus said, "I have no demon in me. For I honor my Father—and you dishonor me. ⁵⁰And though I have no wish to make myself great, God wants this for me and judges [those who reject meᵈ]. ⁵¹With all the earnestness I have I tell you this—no one who obeys me shall ever die!"

---

c. Implied.   d. Implied. Literally, "There is one who seeks and judges."

⁵²The leaders of the Jews said, "Now we know you are possessed by a demon. Even Abraham and the mightiest prophets died, and yet you say that obeying you will keep a man from dying! ⁵³So you are greater than our father Abraham, who died? And greater than the prophets, who died? Who do you think you are?" ⁵⁴Then Jesus told them this: "If I am merely boasting about myself, it doesn't count. But it is my Father—and you claim him as your God—who is saying these glorious things about me. ⁵⁵But you do not even know him. I do. If I said otherwise, I would be as great a liar as you! But it is true—I know him and fully obey him. ⁵⁶Your father Abraham rejoiced to see my day. He knew I was coming and was glad."

⁵⁷*The Jewish leaders:* "You aren't even fifty years old—sure, you've seen Abraham!"

⁵⁸*Jesus:* "The absolute truth is that I was in existence before Abraham was ever born!"

⁵⁹At that point the Jewish leaders picked up stones to kill him. But Jesus was hidden from them, and walked past them and left the Temple.

Cure of the Blind Beggar
Jn 9:1–41

¹As he was walking along, he saw a man blind from birth.

²"Master," his disciples asked him, "why was this man born blind? Was it a result of his own sins or those of his parents?"

³"Neither," Jesus answered. "But to demonstrate the power of God. ⁴All of us must quickly carry out the tasks assigned us by the one who sent me, for there is little time left before the night falls and all work comes to an end. ⁵But while I am

The Jews believed that every affliction was the result of either a person's own sin or that of his or her parents.

still here in the world, I give it my light."

⁶Then he spat on the ground and made mud from the spittle and smoothed the mud over the blind man's eyes, ⁷and told him, "Go and wash in the Pool of Siloam" (the word "Siloam" means "Sent"). So the man went where he was sent and washed and came back seeing!

⁸His neighbors and others who knew him as a blind beggar asked each other, "Is this the same fellow—the beggar?"

⁹Some said yes, and some said no. "It can't be the same man," they thought, "but he surely looks like him!"

And the beggar said, "I *am* the same man!"

¹⁰Then they asked him how in the world he could see. What had happened?

¹¹And he told them, "A man they call Jesus made mud and smoothed it over my eyes and told me to go to the Pool of Siloam and wash off the mud. I did, and I can see!"

¹²"Where is he now?" they asked.

"I don't know," he replied.

¹³Then they took the man to the Pharisees. ¹⁴Now as it happened, this all occurred on a Sabbath.ª ¹⁵Then the Pharisees asked him all about it. So he told them how Jesus had smoothed the mud over his eyes, and when it was washed away, he could see!

¹⁶Some of them said, "Then this fellow Jesus is not from God, because he is working on the Sabbath."

Others said, "But how could an ordinary sinner do such miracles?" So there was a deep division of opinion among them.

This is pure legalism. It was forbidden by law to make clay on the Sabbath.

¹⁷Then the Pharisees turned on the man who had been blind and demanded, "This man who opened your eyes—who do you say he is?"

a. i.e., on Saturday, the weekly Jewish holy day when all work was forbidden.

"I think he must be a prophet sent from God," the man replied.

¹⁸The Jewish leaders wouldn't believe he had been blind, until they called in his parents ¹⁹and asked them, "Is this your son? Was he born blind? If so, how can he see?"

²⁰His parents replied, "We know this is our son and that he was born blind, ²¹but we don't know what happened to make him see, or who did it. He is old enough to speak for himself. Ask him."

²²,²³They said this in fear of the Jewish leaders who had announced that anyone saying Jesus was the Messiah would be excommunicated.

²⁴So for the second time they called in the man who had been blind and told him, "Give the glory to God, not to Jesus, for we know Jesus is an evil person."

²⁵"I don't know whether he is good or bad," the man replied, "but I know this: *I was blind, and now I see!*"

²⁶But what did he do?" they asked. "How did he heal you?"

²⁷"Look!" the man exclaimed. "I told you once; didn't you listen? Why do you want to hear it again? Do you want to become his disciples too?"

²⁸Then they cursed him and said, "You are his disciple, but we are disciples of Moses. ²⁹We know God has spoken to Moses, but as for this fellow, we don't know anything about him."

³⁰"Why, that's very strange!" the man replied. "He can heal blind men, and yet you don't know anything about him! ³¹Well, God doesn't listen to evil men, but he has open ears to those who worship him and do his will. ³²Since the world began there has never been anyone who could open the eyes of someone born blind. ³³If this man were not from God, he couldn't do it."

³⁴"You illegitimate bastard,ᵇ you!" they shouted. "Are you trying to teach *us*?" And they threw him out.

³⁵When Jesus heard what had happened, he found the man and said, "Do you believe in the Messiah?"ᶜ

³⁶The man answered, "Who is he, sir, for I want to."

³⁷"You have seen him," Jesus said, "and he is speaking to you!"

³⁸"Yes, Lord," the man said, "I believe!" And he worshiped Jesus.

³⁹Then Jesus told him, "I have come into the world to give sight to those who are spiritually blind and to show those who think they see that they are blind."

⁴⁰The Pharisees who were standing there asked, "Are you saying we are blind?"

⁴¹"If you were blind, you wouldn't be guilty," Jesus replied. "But your guilt remains because you claim to know what you are doing."

The Good Shepherd
Jn 10:1–21

¹"Anyone refusing to walk through the gate into a sheepfold, who sneaks over the wall, must surely be a thief! ²For a shepherd comes through the gate. ³The gatekeeper opens the gate for him, and the sheep hear his voice and come to him; and he calls his own sheep by name and leads them out. ⁴He walks ahead of them; and they follow him, for they recognize his voice. ⁵They won't follow a stranger but will run from him, for they don't recognize his voice."

⁶Those who heard Jesus use this illustration didn't understand what he meant, ⁷so he ex-

b. Literally, "You were altogether born in sin." c. Literally, "the Son of Man."

plained it to them.

"I am the Gate for the sheep," he said. [8]"All others who came before me were thieves and robbers. But the true sheep did not listen to them. [9]Yes, I am the Gate. Those who come in by way of the Gate will be saved and will go in and out and find green pastures. [10]The thief's purpose is to steal, kill and destroy. My purpose is to give life in all its fullness.

[11]"I am the Good Shepherd. The Good Shepherd lays down his life for the sheep. [12]A hired man will run when he sees a wolf coming and will leave the sheep, for they aren't his and he isn't their shepherd. And so the wolf leaps on them and scatters the flock. [13]The hired man runs because he is hired and has no real concern for the sheep.

[14]"I am the Good Shepherd and know my own sheep, and they know me, [15]just as my Father knows me and I know the Father; and I lay down my life for the sheep. [16]I have other sheep, too, in another fold. I must bring them also, and they will heed my voice; and there will be one flock with one Shepherd.

[17]"The Father loves me because I lay down my life that I may have it back again. [18]No one can kill me without my consent—I lay down my life voluntarily. For I have the right and power to lay it down when I want to and also the right and power to take it again. For the Father has given me this right."

[19]When he said these things, the Jewish leaders were again divided in their opinions about him. [20]Some of them said, "He has a demon or else is crazy. Why listen to a man like that?"

[21]Others said, "This doesn't sound to us like a man possessed by a demon! Can a demon open the eyes of blind men?"

Feast of Dedication
Jn 10:22–42

²²,²³It was winter,ᵃ and Jesus was in Jerusalem at the time of the Dedication Celebration. He was at the Temple, walking through the section known as Solomon's Hall. ²⁴The Jewish leaders surrounded him and asked, "How long are you going to keep us in suspense? If you are the Messiah, tell us plainly."

This feast is also called Hanukkah or Feast of Lights. It occurs in late December.

²⁵"I have already told you,ᵇ and you don't believe me," Jesus replied. "The proof is in the miracles I do in the name of my Father. ²⁶But you don't believe me because you are not part of my flock. ²⁷My sheep recognize my voice, and I know them, and they follow me. ²⁸ I give them eternal life and they shall never perish. No one shall snatch them away from me, ²⁹for my Father has given them to me, and he is more powerful than anyone else, so no one can kidnap them from me. ³⁰I and the Father are one."

³¹Then again the Jewish leaders picked up stones to kill him.

³²Jesus said, "At God's direction I have done many a miracle to help the people. For which one are you killing me?"

³³They replied, "Not for any good work, but for blasphemy; you, a mere man, have declared yourself to be God."

³⁴,³⁵,³⁶"In your own Law it says that men are gods!" he replied. "So if the Scripture, which cannot be untrue, speaks of those as gods to whom the message of God came, do you call it blasphemy when the one sanctified and sent into the world by the Father says, 'I am the Son of God'? ³⁷Don't believe me unless I do miracles of God. ³⁸But if I do, believe them even if you don't believe

a. December 25 was the usual date for this celebration of the cleansing of the Temple.   b. Chapter 5:19; 8:36, 56, 58, etc.

me. Then you will become convinced that the Father is in me, and I in the Father."

³⁹Once again they started to arrest him. But he walked away and left them, ⁴⁰and went beyond the Jordan River to stay near the place where John was first baptizing. ⁴¹And many followed him.

"John didn't do miracles," they remarked to one another, "but all his predictions concerning this man have come true." ⁴²And many came to the decision that he was the Messiah.ᶜ

c. Literally, "Many believed on him there."

11.

BEYOND THE JORDAN

Jesus Again Speaks on Divorce
Mt 19:2-12

²Vast crowds followed him, and he healed their sick. ³Some Pharisees came to interview him, and tried to trap him into saying something that would ruin him.

"Do you permit divorce?" they asked.

⁴"Don't you read the Scriptures?" he replied. "In them it is written that at the beginning God created man and woman, ⁵,⁶and that a man should leave his father and mother, and be forever united to his wife. The two shall become one—no longer two, but one! And no man may divorce what God has joined together."

⁷"Then, why," they asked, "did Moses say a man may divorce his wife by merely writing her a letter of dismissal?"

⁸Jesus replied,"Moses did that in recognition of your hard and evil hearts, but it was not what God had originally intended. ⁹And I tell you this, that anyone who divorces his wife, except for fornication, and marries another, commits adultery."ᵃ

¹⁰Jesus' disciples then said to him, "If that is how it is, it is better not to marry!"

¹¹"Not everyone can accept this statement,"

a. "And the man who marries a divorced woman commits adultery." This sentence is added in some ancient manuscripts.

Jesus said. "Only those whom God helps. [12]Some are born without the ability to marry,[b] and some are disabled by men, and some refuse to marry for the sake of the Kingdom of Heaven. Let anyone who can, accept my statement."

Jesus Blesses Children
Mt 19:13–15

[13]Little children were brought for Jesus to lay his hands on them and pray. But the disciples scolded those who brought them. "Don't bother him," they said.

[14]But Jesus said, "Let the little children come to me, and don't prevent them. For of such is the Kingdom of Heaven." [15]And he put his hands on their heads and blessed them before he left.

The Rich Young Man
Mt 19:16–26

[16]Someone came to Jesus with this question: "Good master, what must I do to have eternal life?"

[17]"When you call me good you are calling me God," Jesus replied, "for God alone is truly good.[c] But to answer your question, you can get to heaven if you keep the commandments."

[18]"Which ones?" the man asked.

And Jesus replied, "Don't kill, don't commit adultery, don't steal, don't lie, [19]honor your father and mother, and love your neighbor as yourself!"

[20]"I've always obeyed every one of them," the youth replied. "What else must I do?"

This account on celibacy and the next incident about the rich young man on poverty concern counsels as distinguished from commandments. All are required to obey commandments while counsels are not necessary for salvation but a way to a higher perfection.

---

b. Literally, "born eunuchs," or "born emasculated."   c. Implied from Lk 18:19.

²¹Jesus told him, "If you want to be perfect, go and sell everything you have and give the money to the poor, and you will have treasure in heaven; and come, follow me." ²²But when the young man heard this, he went away sadly, for he was very rich.

²³Then Jesus said to his disciples, "It is almost impossible for a rich man to get into the Kingdom of Heaven. ²⁴I say it again—it is easier for a camel to go through the eye of a needle than for a rich man to enter the Kingdom of God!"

²⁵This remark confounded the disciples. "Then who in the world can be saved?" they asked.

²⁶Jesus looked at them intently and said, "Humanly speaking, no one. But with God, everything is possible."

Peter's Self-Interest
Mt 19:27–30

²⁷Then Peter said to him, "We left everything to follow you. What will we get out of it?"

²⁸And Jesus replied, "When I, the Messiah,[d] shall sit upon my glorious throne in the Kingdom,[e] you my disciples shall certainly sit on twelve thrones judging the twelve tribes of Israel. ²⁹And anyone who gives up his home, brothers, sisters, father, mother, wife,[f] children, or property, to follow me, shall receive a hundred times as much in return, and shall have eternal life. ³⁰But many who are first now will be last then; and some who are last now will be first then."

The Hypocrisy of the Pharisees
Lk 11:37–54

³⁷,³⁸As he was speaking, one of the Pharisees asked

---

d. Literally, "the Son of Man."   e. Literally, "in the regeneration."   f. Omitted here in many manuscripts, but included in Lk 18:29.

him home for a meal. When Jesus arrived, he sat down to eat without first performing the ceremonial washing required by Jewish custom. This greatly surprised his host.

39Then Jesus said to him, "You Pharisees wash the outside, but inside you are still dirty—full of greed and wickedness! 40Fools! Didn't God make the inside as well as the outside? 41Purity is best demonstrated by generosity.

42"But woe to you Pharisees! For though you are careful to tithe even the smallest part of your income, you completely forget about justice and the love of God. You should tithe, yes, but you should not leave these other things undone.

43"Woe to you Pharisees! For how you love the seats of honor in the synagogues and the respectful greetings from everyone as you walk through the markets! 44Yes, awesome judgment is awaiting you. For you are like hidden graves in a field. Men go by you with no knowledge of the corruption they are passing."

45"Sir," said an expert in religious law who was standing there, "you have insulted my profession, too, in what you just said."

46"Yes," said Jesus, "the same horrors await you! For you crush men beneath impossible religious demands—that you yourselves would never think of trying to keep. 47Woe to you! For you are exactly like your ancestors who killed the prophets long ago. 48Murderers! You agree with your fathers that what they did was right—you would have done the same yourselves.

49"This is what God says about you: 'I will send prophets and apostles to you, and you will kill some of them and chase away the others.'

50"And you of this generation will be held responsible for the murder of God's servants from the founding of the world—[51]from the murder of Abel to the murder of Zechariah who perished between the altar and the sanctuary. Yes, it will surely be charged against you.

[52]"Woe to you experts in religion! For you hide the truth from the people. You won't accept it for yourselves, and you prevent others from having a chance to believe it."

[53,54]The Pharisees and legal experts were furious; and from that time on they plied him fiercely with a host of questions, trying to trap him into saying something for which they could have him arrested.

The lawyers (Scribes) claimed the exclusive right to interpret the Law. Jesus tells them that they do not understand Scripture.

"Beware of These Pharisees"
Lk 12:1–12

[1]Meanwhile the crowds grew until thousands upon thousands were milling about and crushing each other. He turned now to his disciples and warned them, "More than anything else, beware of these Pharisees and the way they pretend to be good when they aren't. But such hypocrisy cannot be hidden forever. [2] It will become as evident as yeast in dough. [3]Whatever they[a] have said in the dark shall be heard in the light, and what you have whispered in the inner rooms shall be broadcast from the housetops for all to hear!

[4]"Dear friends, don't be afraid of these who want to murder you. They can only kill the body; they have no power over your souls. [5]But I'll tell you whom to fear—fear God who has the power to kill and then cast into hell.

[6]"What is the price of five sparrows? A couple of pennies? Not much nore than that. Yet God does not forget a single one of them. [7]And he knows

a. Literally, "you."

the number of hairs on your head! Never fear, you are far more valuable to him than a whole flock of sparrows.

8"And I assure you of this: I, the Messiah,[b] will publicly honor you in the presence of God's angels if you publicly acknowledge me here on earth as your Friend. 9But I will deny before the angels those who deny me here among men. 10(Yet those who speak against me[b] may be forgiven—while those who speak against the Holy Spirit shall never be forgiven.)

11"And when you are brought to trial before these Jewish rulers and authorities in the synagogues, don't be concerned about what to say in your defense, 12for the Holy Spirit will give you the right words even as you are standing there."

Comments on Current Events
Lk 13:1-9

1About this time he was informed that Pilate had butchered some Jews from Galilee as they were sacrificing at the Temple in Jerusalem.

2"Do you think they were worse sinners than other men from Galilee?" he asked. "Is that why they suffered? 3Not at all! And don't you realize that you also will perish unless you leave your evil ways and turn to God?

4"And what about the eighteen men who died when the Tower of Siloam fell on them? Were they the worst sinners in Jerusalem? 5Not at all! And you, too, will perish unless you repent."

6Then he used this illustration: "A man planted a fig tree in his garden and came again and again to see if he could find any fruit on it, but he was always disappointed. 7Finally he told his gardener

These incidents are unrecorded in any history. The Pool of Siloam was south of the Temple. Foundations uncovered in 1914 may be of the tower in question.

b. Literally, "the Son of Man."

to cut it down. 'I've waited three years and there hasn't been a single fig!' he said. 'Why bother with it any longer? It's taking up space we can use for something else.'

⁸"'Give it one more chance,' the gardener answered. 'Leave it another year, and I'll give it special attention and plenty of fertilizer. ⁹If we get figs next year, fine; if not, I'll cut it down.'"

"Don't Heal on the Sabbath"
Lk 13:10–17

¹⁰One Sabbath as he was teaching in a synagogue, ¹¹he saw a seriously handicapped woman who had been bent double for eighteen years and was unable to straighten herself.

¹²Calling her over to him Jesus said, "Woman, you are healed of your sickness!" ¹³He touched her, and instantly she could stand straight. How she praised and thanked God!

¹⁴But the local Jewish leader in charge of the synagogue was very angry about it because Jesus had healed her on the Sabbath day. "There are six days of the week to work," he shouted to the crowd. "Those are the days to come for healing, not on the Sabbath!"

¹⁵But the Lord replied, "You hypocrite! You work on the Sabbath! Don't you untie your cattle from their stalls on the Sabbath and lead them out for water? ¹⁶And is it wrong for me, just because it is the Sabbath day, to free this Jewish woman from the bondage in which Satan has held her for eighteen years?"

¹⁷This shamed his enemies. And all the people rejoiced at the wonderful things he did.

The Narrow Doorway
Lk 13:22–30

²²He went from city to city and village to village, teaching as he went, always pressing onward toward Jerusalem.

²³Someone asked him, "Will only a few be saved?"

And he replied, ²⁴,²⁵"The door to heaven is narrow. Work hard to get in, for the truth is that many will try to enter but when the head of the house has locked the door, it will be too late. Then if you stand outside knocking, and pleading, 'Lord, open the door for us,' he will reply, 'I do not know you.'

²⁶" 'But we ate with you, and you taught in our streets,' you will say.

²⁷"And he will reply, 'I tell you, I don't know you. You can't come in here, guilty as you are. Go away.'

²⁸"And there will be great weeping and gnashing of teeth as you stand outside and see Abraham, Isaac, Jacob, and all the prophets within the Kingdom of God—²⁹for people will come from all over the world to take their places there. ³⁰And note this: some who are despised now will be greatly honored then; and some who are highly thought of now will be least important then."

Jesus spoke of two doors here—one narrow, the other closed.

Prophets Die in Jerusalem
Lk 13:31–35

³¹A few minutes later some Pharisees said to him, "Get out of here if you want to live, for King Herod is after you!"

³²Jesus replied, "Go tell that fox that I will keep on casting out demons and doing miracles of heal-

ing today and tomorrow; and the third day I will reach my destination. ³³Yes, today, tomorrow, and the next day! For it wouldn't do for a prophet of God to be killed except in Jerusalem!

³⁴"O Jerusalem, Jerusalem! The city that murders the prophets. The city that stones those sent to help her. How often I have wanted to gather your children together even as a hen protects her brood under her wings, but you wouldn't let me. ³⁵And now—now your house is left desolate. And you will never again see me until you say, 'Welcome to him who comes in the name of the Lord.'"

Another Sabbath Cure
Lk 14:1–6

¹,²One sabbath as he was in the home of a member of the Jewish Council, the Pharisees were watching him like hawks to see if he would heal a man who was present who was suffering from dropsy.

³Jesus said to the Pharisees and legal experts standing around, "Well, is it within the Law to heal a man on the Sabbath day, or not?"

⁴And when they refused to answer, Jesus took the sick man by the hand and healed him and sent him away.

⁵Then he turned to them: "Which of you doesn't work on the Sabbath?" he asked. "If your cow falls into a pit, don't you proceed at once to get it out?"

⁶Again they had no answer.

Servants of Faith
Lk 17:5–10

⁵One day the apostles said to the Lord, "We need

more faith; tell us how to get it."

⁶"If your faith were only the size of a mustard seed," Jesus answered, "it would be large enough to uproot that mulberry tree over there and send it hurtling into the sea! Your command would bring immediate results! ⁷,⁸,⁹When a servant comes in from plowing or taking care of sheep, he doesn't just sit down and eat, but first prepares his master's meal and serves him his supper before he eats his own. And he is not even thanked, for he is merely doing what he is supposed to do. ¹⁰Just so, if you merely obey me, you should not consider yourselves worthy of praise. For you have simply done your duty!"

Healing of Ten Lepers
Lk 17:11-19

¹¹As they continued onward toward Jerusalem, they reached the border between Galilee and Samaria, ¹²and as they entered a village there, ten lepers stood at a distance, ¹³crying out, "Jesus, sir, have mercy on us!"

¹⁴He looked at them and said, "Go to the Jewish priest and show him that you are healed!" And as they were going, their leprosy disappeared.

¹⁵One of them came back to Jesus, shouting, "Glory to God, I'm healed!"¹⁶ He fell flat on the ground in front of Jesus, face downward in the dust, thanking him for what he had done. This man was a despised[a] Samaritan.

¹⁷Jesus asked, "Didn't I heal ten men? Where are the nine? ¹⁸Does only this foreigner return to give glory to God?"

¹⁹And Jesus said to the man, "Stand up and go; your faith has made you well."

---

a. Implied. Samaritans were despised by Jews as being only "half-breed" Hebrews.

The Approaching Kingdom
Lk 17:20–37

²⁰One day the Pharisees asked Jesus, "When will the Kingdom of God begin?" Jesus replied, "The Kingdom of God isn't ushered in with visible signs. ²¹You won't be able to say, 'It has begun here in this place or there in that part of the country.' For the Kingdom of God is within you."ᵇ

²²Later he talked again about this with his disciples. "The time is coming when you will long for meᶜ to be with you even for a single day, but I won't be here," he said. ²³"Reports will reach you that I have returned and that I am in this place or that; don't believe it or go out to look for me. ²⁴For when I return, you will know it beyond all doubt. It will be as evident as the lightning that flashes across the skies. ²⁵But first I must suffer terribly and be rejected by this whole nation.

²⁶"[When I returnᵈ] the world will be [as indifferent to the things of Godᵈ] as the people were in Noah's day. ²⁷They ate and drank and married—everything just as usual right up to the day when Noah went into the ark and the flood came and destroyed them all.

²⁸"And the world will be as it was in the days of Lot: people went about their daily business—eating and drinking, buying and selling, farming and building—²⁹until the morning Lot left Sodom. Then fire and brimstone rained down from heaven and destroyed them all. ³⁰Yes, it will be 'business as usual' right up to the hour of my return.ᵉ

³¹"Those away from home that day must not return to pack; those in the fields, must not return to town—³²remember what happened to Lot's wife! ³³Whoever clings to his life shall lose it, and whoever loses his life shall save it. ³⁴That night two

---

b. Or, "among you." c. Or, "long for the Son of Man." d. Implied. e. Or, "the hour I am revealed."

men will be asleep in the same room, and one will be taken away, the other left. [35,36]Two women will be working together at household tasks; one will be taken, the other left; and so it will be with men working side by side in the fields."

[37]"Lord, where will they be taken?" the disciples asked.

Jesus replied, "Where the body is, the vultures gather!"[f]

f. This may mean that God's people will be taken out to the execution grounds and their bodies left to the vultures.

12.

CLOSING THE MISSION

Lazarus Dies
Jn 11:1-16

1,2 Do you remember Mary, who poured the costly perfume on Jesus' feet and wiped them with her hair?[a] Well, her brother Lazarus, who lived in Bethany with Mary and her sister Martha, was sick. **3**So the two sisters sent a message to Jesus telling him, "Sir, your good friend is very, very sick."

4But when Jesus heard about it he said, "The purpose of his illness is not death, but for the glory of God. I, the Son of God, will receive glory from this situation."

5Although Jesus was very fond of Martha, Mary, and Lazarus, **6**he stayed where he was for the next two days and made no move to go to them. **7**Finally, after the two days, he said to his disciples, "Let's go to Judea."

8But his disciples objected. "Master," they said, "only a few days ago the Jewish leaders in Judea were trying to kill you. Are you going there again?"

9Jesus replied, "There are twelve hours of daylight every day, and during every hour of it a man can walk safely and not stumble. **10**Only at night is

Lazarus is a shortened form of Eleazar. The disciples did not wish Jesus to return to the area of Jerusalem because of the danger. Lazarus and his sisters must have been a prominent family if the Jewish leaders came out.

a. See Jn 12:3.

there danger of a wrong step, because of the dark." ¹¹Then he said, "Our friend Lazarus has gone to sleep, but now I will go and waken him!"

¹²,¹³The disciples, thinking Jesus meant Lazarus was having a good night's rest, said, "That means he is getting better!" But Jesus meant Lazarus had died.

¹⁴Then he told them plainly, "Lazarus is dead. ¹⁵And for your sake, I am glad I wasn't there, for this will give you another opportunity to believe in me. Come, let's go to him."

¹⁶Thomas, nicknamed "The Twin," said to his fellow disciples, "Let's go too—and die with him."

"I Am the Resurrection"
Jn 11:17–29

¹⁷When they arrived at Bethany, they were told that Lazarus had already been in his tomb for four days. ¹⁸Bethany was only a couple of miles down the road from Jerusalem, ¹⁹and many of the Jewish leaders had come to pay their respects and to console Martha and Mary on their loss. ²⁰When Martha got word that Jesus was coming, she went to meet him. But Mary stayed home.

²¹Martha said to Jesus, "Sir, if you had been here, my brother wouldn't have died. ²²And even now it's not too late, for I know that God will bring my brother back to life again, if you will only ask him to."

²³Jesus told her, "Your brother will come back to life again."

²⁴"Yes," Martha said, "when everyone else does, on Resurrection Day."

²⁵Jesus told her, "I am the one who raises the dead and gives them life again. Anyone who be-

lieves in me, even though he dies like anyone else, shall live again. ²⁶He is given eternal life for believing in me and shall never perish. Do you believe this, Martha?"

²⁷"Yes, Master," she told him. "I believe you are the Messiah, the Son of God, the one we have so long awaited."

²⁸Then she left him and returned to Mary and, calling her aside from the mourners, told her, "He is here and wants to see you." ²⁹So Mary went to him at once.

Jesus Brings Lazarus to Life
Jn 11:30–46

³⁰Now Jesus had stayed outside the village, at the place where Martha met him. ³¹When the Jewish leaders who were at the house trying to console Mary saw her leave so hastily, they assumed she was going to Lazarus' tomb to weep; so they followed her.

³²When Mary arrived where Jesus was, she fell down at his feet, saying, "Sir, if you had been here, my brother would still be alive."

³³When Jesus saw her weeping and the Jewish leaders wailing with her, he was moved with indignation and deeply troubled. ³⁴"Where is he buried?" he asked them.

They told him, "Come and see." ³⁵Tears came to Jesus' eyes.

³⁶"They were close friends," the Jewish leaders said. "See how much he loved him."

³⁷,³⁸But some said, "This fellow healed a blind man—why couldn't he keep Lazarus from dying?" And again Jesus was moved with deep anger. Then they came to the tomb. It was a cave

The Jewish mourning rites lasted for seven days. Thus people would be visiting the family during this period.

with a heavy stone rolled across its door.

³⁹"Roll the stone aside, Jesus told them.

But Martha, the dead man's sister, said, "By now the smell will be terrible, for he has been dead four days."

⁴⁰"But didn't I tell you that you will see a wonderful miracle from God if you believe?"

⁴¹So they rolled the stone aside. Then Jesus looked up to heaven and said, "Father, thank you for hearing me. ⁴²(You always hear me, of course, but I said it because of all these people standing here, so that they will believe you sent me.)" ⁴³Then he shouted, "Lazarus, come out!"

⁴⁴And Lazarus came—bound up in the gravecloth, his face muffled in a head swath. Jesus told them, "Unwrap him and let him go!"

⁴⁵And so at last many of the Jewish leaders who were with Mary and saw it happen, finally believed in him. ⁴⁶But some went away to the Pharisees and reported it to them.

The Plot Against Jesus
Lk 11:47–57

⁴⁷Then the chief priests and Pharisees convened a council to discuss the situation.

"What are we going to do?" they asked each other. "For this man certainly does miracles. ⁴⁸If we let him alone the whole nation will follow him —and then the Roman army will come and kill us and take over the Jewish government."

⁴⁹And one of them, Caiaphas, who was High Priest that year, said, "You stupid idiots—⁵⁰let this one man die for the people—why should the whole nation perish?"

⁵¹This prophecy that Jesus should die for the entire nation came from Caiaphas in his position as High Priest—he didn't think of it by himself, but was inspired to say it. ⁵²It was a prediction that Jesus' death would not be for Israel only, but for all the children of God scattered around the world. ⁵³So from that time on the Jewish leaders began plotting Jesus' death.

⁵⁴Jesus now stopped his public ministry and left Jerusalem; he went to the edge of the desert, to the village of Ephraim, and stayed there with his disciples.

⁵⁵The Passover, a Jewish holy day, was near, and many country people arrived in Jerusalem several days early so that they could go through the cleansing ceremony before the Passover began. ⁵⁶They wanted to see Jesus, and as they gossiped in the Temple, they asked each other, "What do you think? Will he come for the Passover?" ⁵⁷Meanwhile the chief priests and Pharisees had publicly announced that anyone seeing Jesus must report him immediately so that they could arrest him.

Jesus Again Predicts Death
Mk 10:32–34

³²Now they were on the way to Jerusalem, and Jesus was walking along ahead; and as the disciples were following they were filled with terror and dread.

Taking them aside, Jesus once more began describing all that was going to happen to him when they arrived in Jerusalem.

³³"When we get there," he told them, "I, the Messiah,ᵉ will be arrested and taken before the

---

e. Literally, "the Son of Man."

chief priests and the Jewish leaders, who will sentence me to die and hand me over to the Romans to be killed. ³⁴They will mock me and spit on me and flog me with their whips and kill me; but after three days I will come back to life again."

The Mother of James and John
Seeks to Promote Her Sons
Mt 20:20–28

²⁰Then the mother of James and John, the sons of Zebedee, brought them to Jesus and respectfully asked a favor.

²¹"What is your request?" he asked. She replied, "In your Kingdom, will you let my two sons sit on two thrones[c] next to yours?"

²²But Jesus told her, "You don't know what you are asking!" Then he turned to James and John and asked them, "Are you able to drink from the terrible cup I am about to drink from?"

"Yes," they replied, "we are able!"

²³"You shall indeed drink from it," he told them. "But I have no right to say who will sit on the thrones[c] next to mine. Those places are reserved for the persons my Father selects."

²⁴The other ten disciples were indignant when they heard what James and John had asked for.

²⁵But Jesus called them together and said, "Among the heathen, kings are tyrants and each minor official lords it over those beneath him. ²⁶But among you it is quite different. Anyone wanting to be a leader among you must be your servant. ²⁷And if you want to be right at the top, you must serve like a slave. ²⁸Your attitude[d] must be like my own, for I, the Messiah,[e] did not come to be served, but to serve, and to give my life as a ransom for many."

c. Implied.   d. Implied.   e. Literally, "the Son of Man."

Conversion of Zaccheus
Lk 19:1-10

[1,2]As Jesus was passing through Jericho, a man named Zaccheus, one of the most influential Jews in the Roman tax-collecting business (and, of course, a very rich man), [3]tried to get a look at Jesus, but he was too short to see over the crowds. [4]So he ran ahead and climbed into a sycamore tree beside the road, to watch from there.

[5]When Jesus came by he looked up at Zaccheus and called him by name! "Zaccheus!" he said. "Quick! Come down! For I am going to be a guest in your home today!"

[6]Zaccheus hurriedly climbed down and took Jesus to his house in great excitement and joy.

[7]But the crowds were displeased. "He has gone to be the guest of a notorious sinner," they grumbled.

[8]Meanwhile, Zaccheus stood before the Lord and said, "Sir, from now on I will give half my wealth to the poor, and if I find I have overcharged anyone on his taxes, I will penalize myself by giving him back four times as much!"

[9,10]Jesus told him, "This shows[a] that salvation has come to this home today. This man was one of the lost sons of Abraham, and I, the Messiah,[b] have come to search for and to save such souls as his."

Bartimaeus Gets Back His Sight
Mk 10:46-52

[46]And so they reached Jericho. Later, as they left town, a great crowd was following. Now it happened that a blind beggar named Bartimaeus (the son of Timaeus) was sitting beside the road as Jesus was going by.

a. Implied. b. Literally, "the Son of Man."

47When Bartimaeus heard that Jesus from Nazareth was near, he began to shout out, "Jesus, Son of David, have mercy on me!"

48"Shut up!" some of the people yelled at him.

But he only shouted the louder, again and again, "O Son of David, have mercy on me!"

49When Jesus heard him he stopped there in the road and said, "Tell him to come here."

So they called the blind man. "You lucky fellow,"h they said, "come on, he's calling you!" 50Bartimaeus yanked off his old coat and flung it aside, jumped up and came to Jesus.

51"What do you want me to do for you?" Jesus asked.

"O Teacher," the blind man said, "I want to see!"

52And Jesus said to him, "All right, it's done.i Your faith has healed you."

And instantly the blind man could see, and followed Jesus down the road!

Banquet of Simon the Leper
Mt 26:6, Jn 12:2–11

6Jesus now proceeded to Bethany, to the home of Simon the leper. 2A banquet was prepared in Jesus' honor. Martha served, and Lazarus sat at the table with him. 3Then Mary took a jar of costly perfume made from the essence of nard, and anointed Jesus' feet with it and wiped them with her hair. And the house was filled with fragrance.

4But Judas Iscariot, one of his disciples—the one who would betray him—said, 5"That perfume was worth a fortune. It should have been sold and the money given to the poor." 6Not that he cared for the poor, but he was in charge of the disciples'

This Saturday, the eighth of Nisan, begins the last week of Jesus' life.

---

h. Literally, "Be of good cheer."   i. Literally, "Go your way."

funds and often dipped into them for his own use!

⁷Jesus replied, "Let her alone. She did it in preparation for my burial. ⁸You can always help the poor, but I won't be with you very long."

⁹When the ordinary people of Jerusalem heard of his arrival, they flocked to see him and also to see Lazarus—the man who had come back to life again. ¹⁰Then the chief priests decided to kill Lazarus too, ¹¹for it was because of him that many of the Jewish leaders had deserted and believed in Jesus as their Messiah.

13.

THE CONSPIRACY DEVELOPS

Triumphal Entry into Jerusalem
Mt 21:1-9, Lk 19:39-44, Mt 21:10-11,
Jn 12:17-19, Mk 11:11

[1]As Jesus and the disciples approached Jerusalem, and were near the town of Bethpage on the Mount of Olives, Jesus sent two of them into the village ahead.

[2]"Just as you enter," he said, "you will see a donkey tied there, with its colt beside it. Untie them and bring them here. [3]If anyone asks you what you are doing, just say, 'The Master needs them,' and there will be no trouble."

[4]This was done to fulfill the ancient prophecy, [5]"Tell Jerusalem her King is coming to her, riding humbly on a donkey's colt!"

[6]The two disciples did as Jesus said, [7]and brought the animals to him and threw their garments over the colt[a] for him to ride on. [8]And some in the crowd threw down their coats along the road ahead of him, and others cut branches from the trees and spread them out before him.

[9]Then the crowds surged on ahead and pressed along behind, shouting, "God bless King David's Son!"..."God's Man is here![b]...Bless him, Lord!"..."Praise God in highest heaven!"

Bethpage is the first village one reaches leaving Jerusalem for Jericho. It is reached by crossing the Kidron Valley. Events are detailed because of their messianic significance (Zec 14:4, 9:9).

---

a. Implied.   b. Literally, "Blessed is he who comes in the name of the Lord."

³⁹But some of the Pharisees among the crowd said, ''Sir, rebuke your followers for saying things like that!''

⁴⁰He replied, ''If they keep quiet, the stones along the road will burst into cheers!''

⁴¹But as they came closer to Jerusalem and he saw the city ahead, he began to cry. ⁴²''Eternal peace was within your reach and you turned it down,'' he wept, ''and now it is too late. ⁴³Your enemies will pile up earth against your walls and encircle you and close in on you, ⁴⁴and crush you to the ground, and your children within you; your enemies will not leave one stone upon another—for you have rejected the opportunity God offered you.''

¹⁰The entire city of Jerusalem was stirred as he entered. ''Who is this?'' they asked.

¹¹And the crowds replied, ''It's Jesus, the prophet from Nazareth up in Galilee.''

¹⁷And those in the crowd who had seen Jesus call Lazarus back to life were telling all about it. ¹⁸That was the main reason why so many went out to meet him—because they had heard about this mighty miracle.

¹⁹Then the Pharisees said to each other, ''We've lost. Look—the whole world has gone after him!''

¹¹And so he entered Jerusalem and went into the Temple. He looked around carefully at everything and then left—for now it was late in the afternoon—and went out to Bethany with the twelve disciples.

Jesus Drives the Traders from the Temple
Mk 11:12-14, Jn 2:14-22, Mk 11:18-19, Mt 21:17

¹²The next morning as they left Bethany, he felt

hungry. ¹³A little way off he noticed a fig tree in full leaf, so he went over to see if he could find any figs on it. But no, there were only leaves, for it was too early in the season for fruit.

¹⁴Then Jesus said to the tree, "You shall never bear fruit again!" And the disciples heard him say it.

¹⁴In the Temple area he saw merchants selling cattle, sheep, and doves for sacrifices, and money changers behind their counters. ¹⁵Jesus made a whip from some ropes and chased them all out, and drove out the sheep and oxen, scattering the money changers' coins over the floor and turning over their tables! ¹⁶Then, going over to the men selling doves, he told them, "Get these things out of here. Don't turn my Father's House into a market!"

Roman money could not be used in the Temple. It had to be changed for shekels.

¹⁷Then his disciples remembered this prophecy from the Scriptures: "Concern for God's House will be my undoing."

¹⁸What right have you to order them out?" the Jewish leaders[c] demanded. "If you have this authority from God, show us a miracle to prove it."

¹⁹"All right," Jesus replied, "this is the miracle I will do for you: Destroy this sanctuary and in three days I will raise it up!"

²⁰"What!" they exclaimed. "It took forty-six years to build this Temple, and you can do it in three days?" ²¹But by "this sanctuary" he meant his body. ²²After he came back to life again, the disciples remembered his saying this and realized that what he had quoted from the Scriptures really did refer to him, and had all come true!

¹⁸When the chief priests and other Jewish leaders heard what he had done they began planning how best to get rid of him. Their problem was their fear of riots because the people were so en-

---

c. Literally, "the Jews."

thusiastic about Jesus' teaching.

¹⁹That evening as usual they left the city.

¹⁷Then he returned to Bethany, where he stayed overnight.

The Dead Fig Tree
Mk 11:20–25

²⁰Next morning, as the disciples passed the fig tree he had cursed, they saw that it was withered from the roots! ²¹Then Peter remembered what Jesus had said to the tree on the previous day, and exclaimed, "Look, Teacher! The fig tree you cursed has withered!"

²²,²³In reply Jesus said to the disciples, "If you only have faith in God—this is the absolute truth —you can say to this Mount of Olives, 'Rise up and fall into the Mediterranean,' and your command will be obeyed. All that's required is that you really believe and have no doubt! ²⁴Listen to me! You can pray for *anything*, and *if you believe, you have it; it's yours!* ²⁵But when you are praying, first forgive anyone you are holding a grudge against, so that your Father in heaven will forgive you your sins too."

Jesus Refuses an Answer
Mk 11:26–33

²⁶,²⁷,²⁸By this time they had arrived in Jerusalem again, and as he was walking through the Temple area, the chief priests and other Jewish leaders[b] came up to him demanding, "What's going on here? Who gave you the authority to drive out the merchants?"

b. Literally, "scribes and elders."

²⁹Jesus replied, "I'll tell you if you answer one question! ³⁰What about John the Baptist? Was he sent by God, or not? Answer me!"

³¹They talked it over among themselves. "If we reply that God sent him, then he will say, 'All right, why didn't you accept him?' ³²But if we say God didn't send him, then the people will start a riot." (For the people all believed strongly that John was a prophet.)

³³So they said, "We can't answer. We don't know."

To which Jesus replied, "Then I won't answer your question either!"

Jesus Speaks of His Death
Jn 12:20–36

²⁰Some Greeks who had come to Jerusalem to attend the Passover ²¹paid a visit to Philip,ᵃ who was from Bethsaida, and said, "Sir, we want to meet Jesus." ²²Philip told Andrew about it, and they went together to ask Jesus.

²³,²⁴Jesus replied that the time had come for him to return to his glory in heaven, and that "I must fall and die like a kernel of wheat that falls into the furrows of the earth. Unless I die I will be alone—a single seed. But my death will produce many new wheat kernels—a plentiful harvest of new lives. ²⁵If you love your life down here—you will lose it. If you despise your life down here—you will exchange it for eternal glory.

²⁶"If these Greeksᵇ want to be my disciples, tell them to come and follow me, for my servants must be where I am. And if they follow me, the Father will honor them. ²⁷Now my soul is deeply troubled. Shall I pray, 'Father, save me from what

These Greeks were probably Gentiles and not Hellenists (Greek-speaking Jews). They probably picked Philip because of his Greek name. It is not clear whether they came out of sincerity or curiosity.

---

a. Philip's name was Greek, though he was a Jew.   b. Literally, "if any man."

lies ahead'? But this is the very reason why I came! [28]Father, bring glory and honor to your name.''

Then a voice spoke from heaven saying, ''I have already done this, and I will do it again.'' [29]When the crowd heard the voice, some of them thought it was thunder, while others declared an angel had spoken to him.

[30]Then Jesus told them, ''The voice was for your benefit, not mine. [31]The time of judgment for the world has come—and the time when Satan,[c] the prince of this world, shall be cast out. [32]And when I am lifted up [on the cross[d]], I will draw everyone to me.'' [33]He said this to indicate how he was going to die.

[34]''Die?'' asked the crowd. ''We understood that the Messiah would live forever and never die. Why are you saying he will die? What Messiah are you talking about?''

[35]Jesus replied, ''My light will shine out for you just a little while longer. Walk in it while you can, and go where you want to go before the darkness falls, for then it will be too late for you to find your way. [36]Make use of the Light while there is still time; then you will become light bearers.''[e]

The Tax Trap
Mt 22:15–22

[15]Then the Pharisees met together to try to think of some way to trap Jesus into saying something for which they could arrest him. [16]They decided to send some of their men along with the Herodians[b] to ask him this question: ''Sir, we know you are very honest and teach the truth regardless of the consequences, without fear or favor. [17]Now tell

c. Literally, ''prince of this world.'' See 2 Cor 4:4, and Eph 2:2 and 6:12.   d. Implied.   e. Literally, ''sons of light.''

b. The Herodians were a Jewish political party.

us, is it right to pay taxes to the Roman government or not?"

¹⁸But Jesus saw what they were after. "You hypocrites!" he exclaimed. "Who are you trying to fool with your trick questions? ¹⁹Here, show me a coin." And they handed him a penny.

²⁰"Whose picture is stamped on it?" he asked them. "And whose name is this beneath the picture?"

²¹"Caesar's," they replied.

"Well, then, he said, "give it to Caesar if it is his, and give God everything that belongs to God."

²²His reply surprised and baffled them and they went away.

There is political skulduggery here as well as a trap. It was an attempt to turn the Herodians against Jesus. They opposed the Roman rule and hence Roman taxes. The coin probably had the name and likeness of Tiberius Caesar.

The Sadducees on Resurrection
Mt 22:23–46

²³But that same day some of the Sadducees, who say there is no resurrection after death, came to him and asked, ²⁴"Sir, Moses said that if a man died without children, his brother should marry the widow and their children would get all the dead man's property. ²⁵Well, we had among us a family of seven brothers. The first of these men married and then died, without children, so his widow became the second brother's wife. ²⁶This brother also died without children, and the wife was passed to the next brother, and so on until she had been the wife of each of them. ²⁷And then she also died. ²⁸So whose wife will she be in the resurrection? For she was the wife of all seven of them!"

²⁹But Jesus said, "Your error is caused by your ignorance of the Scriptures and of God's power!

The Sadducees were very conservative, representing the priestly and landowner classes. The Law was the basis of their religion and since Mosaic Law did not mention the resurrection, they denied it.

³⁰For in the resurrection there is no marriage; everyone is as the angels in heaven. ³¹But now, as to whether there is a resurrection of the dead—don't you ever read the Scriptures? Don't you realize that God was speaking directly to you when he said, ³²'I *am* the God of Abraham, Isaac, and Jacob'? So God is not the God of the dead, but of the *living*.''ᶜ

³³The crowds were profoundly impressed by his answers—³⁴,³⁵but not the Pharisees! When they heard that he had routed the Sadducees with his reply, they thought up a fresh question of their own to ask him.

One of them, a lawyer, spoke up: ³⁶''Sir, which is the most important command in the laws of Moses?''

³⁷Jesus replied, '''Love the Lord your God with all your heart, soul, and mind.' ³⁸,³⁹This is the first and greatest commandment. The second most important is similar: 'Love your neighbor as much as you love yourself.' ⁴⁰All the other commandments and all the demands of the prophets stem from these two laws and are fulfilled if you obey them. Keep only these and you will find that you are obeying all the others.''

⁴¹Then, surrounded by the Pharisees, he asked them a question: ⁴²''What about the Messiah? Whose son is he?'' ''The son of David,'' they replied.

⁴³''Then why does David, speaking under the inspiration of the Holy Spirit, call him 'Lord'?'' Jesus asked. ''For David said, ⁴⁴'God said to my Lord, Sit at my right hand until I put your enemies beneath your feet.' ⁴⁵Since David called him 'Lord,' how can he be merely his son?''

⁴⁶They had no answer. And after that no one dared ask him any more questions.

---

c. I.e., if Abraham, Isaac, and Jacob, long dead, were not alive in the presence of God, then God would have said, ''I *was* the God of Abraham, etc.''

Jesus Condemns the Jewish Establishment
Mt 23:1–36

¹Then Jesus said to the crowds, and to his disciples, ²"You would think these Jewish leaders and these Pharisees were Moses, the way they keep making up so many laws!ᵃ ³And of course you should obey their every whim! It may be all right to do what they say, but above anything else, *don't follow their example.* For they don't do what they tell you to do. ⁴They load you with impossible demands that they themselves don't even try to keep.

⁵"Everything they do is done for show. They act holyᵇ by wearing on their arms little prayer boxes with Scripture verses inside,ᶜ and by lengthening the memorial fringes of their robes. ⁶And how they love to sit at the head table at banquets, and in the reserved pews in the synagogue! ⁷How they enjoy the deference paid them on the streets, and to be called 'Rabbi' and 'Master'! ⁸Don't ever let anyone call you that. For only God is your Rabbi and all of you are on the same level, as brothers. ⁹And don't address anyone here on earth as 'Father,' for only God in heaven should be addressed like that. ¹⁰And don't be called 'Master,' for only one is your master, even the Messiah.

¹¹"The more lowly your service to others, the greater you are. To be the greatest, be a servant. ¹²But those who think themselves great shall be disappointed and humbled; and those who humble themselves shall be exalted.

¹³,¹⁴"Woe to you, Pharisees, and you other religious leaders. Hypocrites! For you won't let others enter the Kingdom of Heaven, and won't go in yourselves. And you pretend to be holy, with all your long, public prayers in the streets,

---

a. Literally, "sit on Moses' seat."   b. Implied.   c. Literally, "enlarge their phylacteries."

while you are evicting widows from their homes. Hypocrites! [15]Yes, woe upon you hypocrites. For you go to all lengths to make one convert, and then turn him into twice the son of hell you are yourselves. [16]Blind guides! Woe upon you! For your rule is that to swear 'By God's Temple' means nothing—you can break that oath, but to swear 'By the gold in the Temple' is binding! [17]Blind fools! Which is greater, the gold, or the Temple that sanctifies the gold? [18]And you say that to take an oath 'By the altar' can be broken, but to swear 'By the gifts on the altar' is binding! [19]Blind! For which is greater, the gift on the altar, or the altar itself that sanctifies the gift? [20]When you swear 'By the altar' you are swearing by it and everything on it, [21]and when you swear 'By the Temple' you are swearing by it, and by God who lives in it. [22]And when you swear 'By heavens' you are swearing by the Throne of God and by God himself.

[23]"Yes, woe upon you, Pharisees, and you other religious leaders—hypocrites! For you tithe down to the last mint leaf in your garden, but ignore the important things—justice and mercy and faith. Yes, you should tithe, but you shouldn't leave the more important things undone. [24]Blind guides! You strain out a gnat and swallow a camel.

[25]"Woe to you, Pharisees, and you religious leaders—hypocrites! You are so careful to polish the outside of the cup, but the inside is foul with extortion and greed. [26]Blind Pharisees! First cleanse the inside of the cup, and then the whole cup will be clean.

[27]"Woe to you, Pharisees, and you religious leaders! You are like beautiful mausoleums—full of dead men's bones, and of foulness and corruption. [28]You try to look like saintly men, but under-

neath those pious robes of yours are hearts be-smirched with every sort of hypocrisy and sin.

²⁹,³⁰"Yes, woe to you, Pharisees, and you religious leaders—hypocrites! For you build monuments to the prophets killed by your fathers and lay flowers on the graves of the godly men they destroyed, and say, 'We certainly would never have acted as our fathers did.'

³¹"In saying that, you are accusing yourselves of being the sons of wicked men. ³²And you are following in their steps, filling up the full measure of their evil. ³³Snakes! Sons of vipers! How shall you escape the judgment of hell?

³⁴"I will send you prophets, and wise men, and inspired writers, and you will kill some by crucifixion, and rip open the backs of others with whips in your synagogues, and hound them from city to city, ³⁵so that you will become guilty of all the blood of murdered godly men from righteous Abel to Zechariah (son of Barachiah), slain by you in the Temple between the altar and the sanctuary. ³⁶Yes all the accumulated judgment of the centuries shall break upon the heads of this very generation."

Abel was the first victim of murder in the Bible. Zechariah was the last prophet killed in the Hebrew Bible (2 Chr 24:2-22).

The Widow's Last Penny
Mk 12:41-44

⁴¹Then he went over to the collection boxes in the Temple and sat and watched as the crowds dropped in their money. Some who were rich put in large amounts. ⁴²Then a poor widow came and dropped in two pennies.

⁴³,⁴⁴He called his disciples to him and remarked, "That poor widow has given more than all those rich men put together! For they gave a little of their extra fat,ᶜ while she gave up her last penny."

---

c. Literally, "out of their surplus."

The Ruin of the Temple
Mk 13:1–2

¹As he was leaving the Temple that day, one of his disciples said, "Teacher, what beautiful buildings these are! Look at the decorated stonework on the walls."

²Jesus replied, "Yes, look! For not one stone will be left upon another, except as ruins."

Herod's restoration of the temple was practically complete. It was truly a magnificent structure as a model in Jerusalem today shows. Except for the west wall, it was entirely leveled by the Romans in A.D. 70.

The Sermon on the End of the World
Mk 13:3–10, Lk 21:12–19, Mk 13:14–23, Mt 24:26–31, Mk 13:28–31, Mt 24:36–42, Lk 21:34–36, Mt 25:31–46

^{3,4}And as he sat on the slopes of the Mount of Olives across the valley from Jerusalem, Peter, James, John, and Andrew got alone with him and asked him, "Just when is all this going to happen to the Temple? Will there be some warning ahead of time?"

⁵So Jesus launched into an extended reply. "Don't let anyone mislead you," he said, ⁶"for many will come declaring themselves to be your Messiah, and will lead many astray. ⁷And wars will break out near and far, but this is not the signal of the end-time.

⁸"For nations and kingdoms will proclaim war against each other, and there will be earthquakes in many lands, and famines. These herald only the early stages of the anguish ahead. ⁹But when these things begin to happen, watch out! For you will be in great danger. You will be dragged before the courts, and beaten in the synagogues, and accused before governors and kings of being my followers. This is your opportunity to tell them the Good News. ¹⁰And the Good News must first be

made known in every nation before the end-time finally comes.[a]

¹²"But before all this occurs, there will be a time of special persecution, and you will be dragged into synagogues and prisons and before kings and governors for my name's sake. ¹³But as a result, the Messiah will be widely known and honored.[b] ¹⁴Therefore, don't be concerned about how to answer the charges against you, ¹⁵for I will give you the right words and such logic that none of your opponents will be able to reply! ¹⁶Even those closest to you—your parents, brothers, relatives, and friends will betray you and have you arrested; and some of you will be killed. ¹⁷And everyone will hate you because you are mine and are called by my name. ¹⁸But not a hair of your head will perish! ¹⁹For if you stand firm, you will win your souls.

¹⁴"When you see the horrible thing standing in the Temple[b]—reader, pay attention!—flee, if you can, to the Judean hills. ¹⁵,¹⁶Hurry! If you are on your rooftop porch, don't even go back into the house. If you are out in the fields, don't even return for your money or clothes.

¹⁷"Woe to pregnant women in those days, and to mothers nursing their children. ¹⁸And pray that your flight will not be in winter. ¹⁹For those will be days of such horror as have never been since the beginning of God's creation, nor will ever be again. ²⁰And unless the Lord shortens that time of calamity, not a soul in all the earth will survive. But for the sake of his chosen ones he will limit those days.

²¹"And then if anyone tells you, 'This is the Messiah,' or, 'That one is,' don't pay any attention. ²²For there will be many false Messiahs and false prophets who will do wonderful miracles

In the preceding discourse and in this, Jesus seems to have in mind the destruction of Jerusalem in A.D. 70.

---

a. Implied.

b. Literally, "standing where he ought not."

that would deceive, if possible, even God's own children.ᶜ ²³Take care! I have warned you!

²⁶"So if someone tells you the Messiah has returned and is out in the desert, don't bother to go and look. Or, that he is hiding at a certain place, don't believe it! ²⁷For as the lightning flashes across the sky from east to west, so shall my coming be, when I, the Messiah,ʰ return. ²⁸And wherever the carcass is, there the vultures will gather.

²⁹"Immediately after the persecution of those days the sun will be darkened, and the moon will not give light, and the stars will seemⁱ to fall from the heavens, and the powers overshadowing the earth will be convulsed.ʲ

³⁰"And then at last the signal of my comingᵏ will appear in the heavens and there will be deep mourning all around the earth. And the nations of the world will see me arrive in the clouds of heaven, with power and great glory. ³¹And I shall send forth my angels with the sound of a mighty trumpet blast, and they shall gather my chosen ones from the farthest ends of the earth and heaven.ˡ

²⁸"Now, here is a lesson from a fig tree. When its buds become tender and its leaves begin to sprout, you know that spring has come. ²⁹And when you see these things happening that I've described, you can be sure that my return is very near, that I am right at the door.

³⁰"Yes, these are the events that will signal the end of the age.ᵉ ³¹Heaven and earth shall disappear, but my words stand sure forever. ³⁶But no one knows the date and hour when the end will be —not even the angels. No, nor even God's Son.ᵒ Only the Father knows.

c. Literally, "elect of God."

h. Literally, "the Son of Man." i. Literally, "the stars shall fall from heaven." j. Literally, "the powers of the heavens shall be shaken." See Eph 6:12. k. Literally, "of the coming of the Son of Man." l. "From the four winds, from one end of heaven to the other."

e. Literally, "of this generation."

o. Literally, "neither the Son." Many ancient manuscripts omit this phrase.

37,38 "The world will be at ease[p]—banquets and parties and weddings—just as it was in Noah's time before the sudden coming of the flood; 39people wouldn't believe[q] what was going to happen until the flood actually arrived and took them all away. So shall my coming be.

40 "Two men will be working together in the fields, and one will be taken, the other left. 41Two women will be going about their household tasks; one will be taken, the other left.

42 "So be prepared, for you don't know what day your Lord is coming.

34,35 "Watch out! Don't let my sudden coming catch you unawares; don't let me find you living in careless ease, carousing and drinking, and occupied with the problems of this life, like all the rest of the world. 36Keep a constant watch. And pray that if possible you may arrive in my presence without having to experience these horrors. g

31 "But when I, the Messiah,[e] shall come in my glory, and all the angels with me, then I shall sit upon my throne of glory. 32And all the nations shall be gathered before me. And I will separate the people[f] as a shepherd separates the sheep from the goats, 33and place the sheep at my right hand, and the goats at my left.

34 "Then I, the King, shall say to those at my right, 'Come, blessed of my Father, into the Kingdom prepared for you from the founding of the world. 35For I was hungry and you fed me; I was thirsty and you gave me water; I was a stranger and you invited me into your homes; 36naked and you clothed me; sick and in prison, and you visited me.'

37 "Then these righteous ones will reply, 'Sir, when did we ever see you hungry and feed you? Or thirsty and give you anything to drink? 38Or a

p. Implied.   q. Literally, "knew not."

g. Or, "Pray for strength to pass safely through these coming horrors."

e. Literally, "the Son of Man."   f. Or, "separate the nations."

stranger, and help you? Or naked, and clothe you? ³⁹When did we ever see you sick or in prison, and visit you?'

⁴⁰"And I, the King, will tell them, 'When you did it to these my brothers you were doing it to me!' ⁴¹Then I will turn to those on my left and say, 'Away with you, you cursed ones, into the eternal fire prepared for the devil and his demons. ⁴²For I was hungry and you wouldn't feed me; thirsty, and you wouldn't give me anything to drink; ⁴³a stranger, and you refused me hospitality; naked, and you wouldn't clothe me; sick, and in prison, and you didn't visit me.'

⁴⁴"Then they will reply, 'Lord, when did we ever see you hungry or thirsty or a stranger or naked or sick or in prison, and not help you?'

⁴⁵"And I will answer, 'When you refused to help the least of these my brothers, you were refusing help to me.'

⁴⁶"And they shall go away into eternal punishment; but the righteous into everlasting life."

The Plot Is Formed
Mt 26:1–5

¹When Jesus had finished this talk with his disciples, he told them,

²"As you know, the Passover celebration begins in two days, and Iᵃ shall be betrayed and crucified."

³At that very moment the chief priests and other Jewish officials were meeting at the residence of Caiaphas the High Priest, ⁴to discuss ways of capturing Jesus quietly, and killing him. ⁵"But not during the Passover celebration," they agreed, "for there would be a riot."

Joseph Caiaphas was high priest from A.D. 18–36. He was the son-in-law of Annas, former high priest. Annas still held great influence. They were both wealthy men since they controlled the trading booths in the Temple.

a. Literally, "the Son of Man."

Judas Agrees to Betray Jesus
Mt 26:14–16

¹⁴Then Judas Iscariot, one of the twelve apostles, went to the chief priests, ¹⁵and asked, "How much will you pay me to get Jesus into your hands?" And they gave him thirty silver coins. ¹⁶From that time on, Judas watched for an opportunity to betray Jesus to them.

A silver shekel was worth about one dollar. Therefore, the price for betraying Jesus was thirty dollars.

14.

THE LAST SUPPER

Preparation for the Seder
Lk 22:1–2, Mt 26:17, Lk 22:8–13

¹And now the Passover celebration was drawing near—the Jewish festival when only bread made without yeast was used. ²The chief priests and other religious leaders were actively plotting Jesus' murder, trying to find a way to kill him without starting a riot—a possibility they greatly feared.

¹⁷On the first day of the Passover ceremonies, when bread made with yeast was purged from every Jewish home, the disciples came to Jesus and asked, "Where shall we plan to eat the Passover?"

⁸Jesus sent Peter and John ahead to find a place to prepare their Passover meal.

⁹"Where do you want us to go?" they asked.

¹⁰And he replied, "As soon as you enter Jerusalem,ᵃ you will see a man walking along carrying a pitcher of water. Follow him into the house he enters, ¹¹and say to the man who lives there, 'Our Teacher says for you to show us the guest room where he can eat the Passover meal with his disciples.' ¹²He will take you upstairs to a large room all ready for us. That is the place. Go ahead and prepare the meal there."

---

a. Literally, "the city."

¹³They went off to the city and found everything just as Jesus had said, and prepared the Passover supper.

Jesus Teaches Humility
Lk 22:14–16, 24–30; Jn 13:1–17

¹⁴Then Jesus and the others arrived, and at the proper time all sat down together at the table; ¹⁵and he said, 'I have looked forward to this hour with deep longing, anxious to eat this Passover meal with you before my suffering begins. ¹⁶For I tell you now that I won't eat it again until what it represents has occurred in the Kingdom of God.''

²⁴And they began to argue among themselves as to who would have the highest rank [in the coming Kingdom[d]].

²⁵Jesus told them, "In this world the kings and great men order their slaves around, and the slaves have no choice but to like it![e] ²⁶But among you, the one who serves you best will be your leader. ²⁷Out in the world the master sits at the table and is served by his servants. But not here! For I am your servant. ²⁸Nevertheless, because you have stood true to me in these terrible days,[f] ²⁹and because my Father has granted me a Kingdom, I, here and now, grant you the right ³⁰to eat and drink at my table in that Kingdom; and you will sit on thrones judging the twelve tribes of Israel.''

¹,²,³Jesus knew on the evening of Passover Day that it would be his last night on earth before returning to his Father. During supper the devil had already suggested to Judas Iscariot, Simon's son, that this was the night to carry out his plan to betray Jesus. Jesus knew that the Father had given

Judas had evidently not as yet decided on the moment of betrayal. John now tells us that it was ''during supper.''

---

d. Implied.   e. Literally, ''they (the kings and great men) are called 'benefactors.''' f. Literally, ''you have continued with me in my temptation.''

him everything and that he had come from God and would return to God. And how he loved his disciples! 4So he got up from the supper table, took off his robe, wrapped a towel around his loins,ª 5poured water into a basin, and began to wash the disciples' feet and to wipe them with the towel he had around him.

6When he came to Simon Peter, Peter said to him, "Master, you shouldn't be washing our feet like this!"

7Jesus replied, "You don't understand now why I am doing it; some day you will."

8"No," Peter protested, "you shall never wash my feet!"

"But if I don't, you can't be my partner," Jesus replied.

9Simon Peter exclaimed, "Then wash my hands and head as well—not just my feet!"

10Jesus replied, "One who has bathed all over needs only to have his feet washed to be entirely clean. Now you are clean—but that isn't true of everyone here. 11For Jesus knew who would betray him. That is what he meant when he said, "Not all of you are clean."

12After washing their feet he put on his robe again and sat down and asked, "Do you understand what I was doing? 13You call me 'Master' and 'Lord,' and you do well to say it, for it is true. 14And since I, the Lord and Teacher, have washed your feet, you ought to wash each other's feet. 15I have given you an example to follow: do as I have done to you. 16How true it is that a servant is not greater than his master. Nor is the messenger more important than the one who sends him. 17You know these things—now do them! That is the path of blessing."

This is Jesus' answer to the dispute on precedence.

---

a. As the lowliest of slaves would dress.

Jesus Names Judas as His Betrayer
Jn 13:18–21, Mt 26:22–24, Jn 13:22–30

18"I am not saying these things to all of you; I know so well each one of you I chose. The Scripture declares, 'One who eats supper with me will betray me,' and this will soon come true. 19I tell you this now so that when it happens, you will believe on me.

20"Truly, anyone welcoming my messenger is welcoming me. And to welcome me is to welcome the Father who sent me."

21Now Jesus was in great anguish of spirit and exclaimed, "Yes, it is true—one of you will betray me."

22Sorrow chilled their hearts, and each one asked, "Am I the one?" 23He replied, "It is the one I served first.b 24For I must diec just as was prophesied, but woe to the man by whom I am betrayed. Far better for that one if he had never been born."

22The disciples looked at each other, wondering whom he could mean. 23Since Ib was sitting nextc to Jesus at the table, being his closest friend, 24Simon Peter motioned to me to ask him who it was who would do this terrible deed.

25So I turnedd and asked him, "Lord, who is it?"

26He told me, "It is the one I honor by giving the bread dipped in the sauce."e

And when he had dipped it, he gave it to Judas, son of Simon Iscariot.

27As soon as Judas had eaten it, Satan entered into him. Then Jesus told him, "Hurry—do it now."

28None of the others at the table knew what Jesus meant. 29Some thought that since Judas was

b. Literally, "he that dipped his hand with me in the dish."   c. Literally, "the Son of Man goes."

b. Literally, "there was one at the table." All commentators believe him to be John, the writer of this book. c. Literally, "reclining on Jesus' bosom." The custom of the period was to recline around the table, leaning on the left elbow. John, next to Jesus, was at his side.   d. Literally, "leaning back against Jesus' chest," to whisper his inquiry.   e. Literally, "He it is for whom I shall dip the sop and give it him." The honored guest was thus singled out in the custom of that time.

their treasurer, Jesus was telling him to go and pay for the food or to give some money to the poor. ³⁰Judas left at once, going out into the night.

The New Commandment
Jn 13:31–35

³¹As soon as Judas left the room, Jesus said, "My time has come; the glory of God will soon surround me—and God shall receive great praise because of all that happens to me. ³²And God shall give me his own glory, and this so very soon. ³³Dear, dear children, how brief are these moments before I must go away and leave you! Then, though you search for me, you cannot come to me —just as I told the Jewish leaders.

³⁴"And so I am giving a new commandment to you now—love each other just as much as I love you. ³⁵Your strong love for each other will prove to the world that you are my disciples."

The Institution of the Memorial
Mt 26:26–28

²⁶As they were eating, Jesus took a small loaf of bread and blessed it and broke it apart and gave it to the disciples and said, "Take it and eat it, for this is my body."

²⁷And he took a cup of wine and gave thanks for it and gave it to them and said, "Each one drink from it, ²⁸for this is my blood, sealing the New Covenant. It is poured out to forgive the sins of multitudes. ²⁹Mark my words—I will not drink this wine again until the day I drink it new with you in my Father's Kingdom."

Betrayal of the Apostles
Mt 26:31–35, Jn 13:36–37, Lk 22:31–38

³¹Then Jesus said to them, "Tonight you will all desert me. For it is written in the Scriptures[d] that God will smite the Shepherd, and the sheep of the flock will be scattered. ³²But after I have been brought back to life again I will go to Galilee, and meet you there."

³³Peter declared, "If everyone else deserts you, I won't."

³⁴Jesus told him, "The truth is that this very night, before the cock crows at dawn, you will deny me three times!"

³⁵"I would die first!" Peter insisted. And all the other disciples said the same thing.

³⁶Simon Peter said, "Master, where are you going?"

And Jesus replied, "You can't go with me now; but you will follow me later."

³⁷"But why can't I come now?" he asked, "For I am ready to die for you."

³¹"Simon, Simon, Satan has asked to have you, to sift you like wheat, ³²but I have pleaded in prayer for you that your faith should not completely fail.[g] So when you have repented and turned to me again, strengthen and build up the faith of your brothers."

³³Simon said, "Lord, I am ready to go to jail with you, and even to die with you."

³⁴But Jesus said, "Peter, let me tell you something. Between now and tomorrow morning when the rooster crows, you will deny me three times, declaring that you don't even know me."

³⁵Then Jesus asked them, "When I sent you out to preach the Good News and you were without money, duffle bag, or extra clothing, how did you

d. Zechariah 13:7.

g. Literally, "fail not."

get along?''

"Fine," they replied.

[36]"But now," he said, "take a duffle bag if you have one, and your money. And if you don't have a sword, better sell your clothes and buy one! [37]For the time has come for this prophecy about me to come true: 'He will be condemned as a criminal!' Yes, everything written about me by the prophets will come true."

[38]"Master," they replied, "we have two swords among us."

"Enough!" he said.

Jesus is speaking figuratively—"Be prepared." Peter takes Him literally.

Jesus and the Father Are One
Jn 14:1-14

[1]"Let not your heart be troubled. You are trusting God, now trust in me. [2,3]There are many homes up there where my Father lives, and I am going to prepare them for your coming. When everything is ready, then I will come and get you, so that you can always be with me where I am. If this weren't so, I would tell you plainly. [4]And you know where I am going and how to get there."

[5]"No, we don't," Thomas said. "We haven't any idea where you are going, so how can we know the way?"

[6]Jesus told him, "I am the Way—yes, and the Truth and the Life. No one can get to the Father except by means of me. [7]If you had known who I am, then you would have known who my Father is. From now on you know him—and have seen him!"

[8]Philip said, "Sir, show us the Father and we will be satisfied."

[9]Jesus replied, "Don't you even yet know who I am, Philip, even after all this time I have been with

you? Anyone who has seen me has seen the Father! So why are you asking to see him? [10]Don't you believe that I am in the Father and the Father is in me? The words I say are not my own but are from my Father who lives in me. And he does his work through me. [11]Just believe it—that I am in the Father and the Father is in me. Or else believe it because of the mighty miracles you have seen me do.

[12,13]"In solemn truth I tell you, anyone believing in me shall do the same miracles I have done, and even greater ones, because I am going to be with the Father. You can ask him for *anything*, using my name, and I will do it, for this will bring praise to the Father because of what I, the Son, will do for you. [14]Yes, ask *anything*, using my name, and I will do it!"

Promise of the Holy Spirit
Jn 14:15–31

[15,16]"If you love me, obey me; and I will ask the Father and he will give you another Comforter, and he will never leave you. [17]He is the Holy Spirit, the Spirit who leads into all truth. The world at large cannot receive him, for it isn't looking for him, and doesn't recognize him. But you do, for he lives with you now and some day shall be in you. [18]No, I will not abandon you or leave you as orphans in the storm—I will come to you. [19]In just a little while I will be gone from the world, but I will still be present with you. For I will live again—and you will too. [20]When I come back to life again, you will know that I am in my Father, and you in me, and I in you. [21]The one who obeys me is the one who loves me; and because he loves

me, my Father will love him; and I will too, and I will reveal myself to him.''

²²Judas (not Judas Iscariot, but his other disciple with that name) said to him, ''Sir, why are you going to reveal yourself only to us disciples and not to the world at large?''

²³Jesus replied, ''Because I will only reveal myself to those who love me and obey me. The Father will love them too, and we will come to them and live with them. ²⁴Anyone who doesn't obey me doesn't love me. And remember, I am not making up this answer to your question! It is the answer given by the Father who sent me. ²⁵I am telling you these things now while I am still with you. ²⁶But when the Father sends the Comforterᵃ instead of meᵇ—and by the Comforter I mean the Holy Spirit—he will teach you much, as well as remind you of everything I myself have told you.

²⁷''I am leaving you with a gift—peace of mind and heart! And the peace I give isn't fragile like the peace the world gives. So don't be troubled or afraid.ᶜ ²⁸Remember what I told you—I am going away, but I will come back to you again. If you really love me, you will be very happy for me, for now I can go to the Father, who is greater than I am. ²⁹I have told you these things before they happen so that when they do, you will believe [in meᶜ].

³⁰''I don't have much more time to talk to you, for the evil prince of this world approaches. He has no power over me, ³¹but I will freely do what the Father requires of me so that the world will know that I love the Father.''

''I Am the Vine''
Jn 15:1–8

¹''I am the true Vine, and my Father is the Gar-

---

a. Or, ''Helper.''   b. Literally, ''in my name.''   c. Implied.

dener. [2]He lops off every branch that doesn't produce. And he prunes those branches that bear fruit for even larger crops. [3]He has already tended you by pruning you back for greater strength and usefulness by means of the commands I gave you. [4]Take care to live in me, and let me live in you. For a branch can't produce fruit when severed from the vine. Nor can you be fruitful apart from me.

[5]"Yes, I am the Vine, you are the branches. Whoever lives in me and I in him shall produce a large crop of fruit. For apart from me you can't do a thing. [6]If anyone separates from me, he is thrown away like a useless branch, withers, and is gathered into a pile with all the others and burned. [7]But if you stay in me and obey my commands, you may ask any request you like, and it will be granted! [8]My true disciples produce bountiful harvests. This brings great glory to my Father."

The Measure of Love
Jn 15:9–15

[9]"I have loved you even as the Father has loved me. Live within my love. [10]When you obey me you are living in my love, just as I obey my Father and live in his love. [11]I have told you this so that you will be filled with my joy. Yes, your cup of joy will overflow! [12]I demand that you love each other as much as I love you. [13]And here is how to measure it—the greatest love is shown when a person lays down his life for his friends; [14]and you are my friends if you obey me. [15]I no longer call you slaves, for a master doesn't confide in his slaves; now you are my friends, proved by the fact that I have told you everything the Father told me."

"I Chose You!"
Jn 15:16–27

¹⁶"You didn't choose me! I chose you! I appointed you to go and produce lovely fruit always, so that no matter what you ask for from the Father, using my name, he will give it to you. ¹⁷I demand that you love each other, ¹⁸for you get enough hate from the world! But then, it hated me before it hated you. ¹⁹The world would love you if you belonged to it; but you don't—for I chose you to come out of the world, and so it hates you. ²⁰Do you remember what I told you? 'A slave isn't greater than his master!' So since they persecuted me, naturally they will persecute you. And if they had listened to me, they would listen to you! ²¹The people of the world will persecute you because you belong to me, for they don't know God who sent me.

²²"They would not be guilty if I had not come and spoken to them. But now they have no excuse for their sin. ²³Anyone hating me is also hating the Father. ²⁴If I hadn't done such mighty miracles among them they would not be counted guilty. But as it is, they saw these miracles and yet they hated both of us—me and my Father. ²⁵This has fulfilled what the prophets said concerning the Messiah, 'They hated me without reason.'

²⁶"But I will send you the Comforter—the Holy Spirit, the source of all truth. He will come to you from the Father and will tell you all about me. ²⁷And you also must tell everyone about me, because you have been with me from the beginning."

Again, the Promise
Jn 16:1–16

¹"I have told you these things so that you won't be staggered [by all that lies ahead.ª] ²For you will be excommunicated from the synagogues, and indeed the time is coming when those who kill you will think they are doing God a service. ³This is because they have never known the Father or me. ⁴Yes, I'm telling you these things now so that when they happen you will remember I warned you. I didn't tell you earlier because I was going to be with you for a while longer.

⁵"But now I am going away to the one who sent me; and none of you seems interested in the purpose of my going; none wonders why.ᵇ ⁶Instead you are only filled with sorrow. ⁷But the fact of the matter is that it is best for you that I go away, for if I don't, the Comforter won't come. If I do, he will—for I will send him to you.

⁸"And when he has come he will convince the world of its sins, and of the availability of God's goodness, and of deliverance from judgment.ᶜ ⁹The world's sin is unbelief in me; ¹⁰there is righteousness available because I go to the Father and you shall see me no more; ¹¹there is deliverance from judgment because the prince of this world has already been judged.

¹²"Oh, there is so much more I want to tell you, but you can't understand it now. ¹³When the Holy Spirit, who is truth, comes, he shall guide you into all truth, for he will not be presenting his own ideas, but will be passing on to you what he has heard. He will tell you about the future. ¹⁴He shall praise me and bring me great honor by showing you my glory. ¹⁵All the Father's glory is mine; this is what I mean when I say that he will show you

a. Implied.   b. Literally, "none of you is asking me whither I am going." The question had been asked before (Jn 13:36, 14:5), but apparently not in this deeper sense.   c. Literally, "he will convict the world of sin and righteousness and judgment."

my glory. [16]In just a little while I will be gone, and you will see me no more; but just a little while after that, and you will see me again!''

"Pray in My Name"
Jn 16:17–33

[17,18]''Whatever is he saying?'' some of his disciples asked. ''What is this about 'going to the Father'? We don't know what he means.''

[19]Jesus realized they wanted to ask him so he said, ''Are you asking yourselves what I mean? [20]The world will greatly rejoice over what is going to happen to me, and you will weep. But your weeping shall suddenly be turned to wonderful joy [when you see me again[d]]. [21]It will be the same joy as that of a woman in labor when her child is born—her anguish gives place to rapturous joy and the pain is forgotten. [22]You have sorrow now, but I will see you again and then you will rejoice; and no one can rob you of that joy. [23]At that time you won't need to ask me for anything, for you can go directly to the Father and ask him, and he will give you what you ask for because you use my name. [24]You haven't tried this before, [but begin now[d]]. Ask, using my name, and you will receive, and your cup of joy will overflow.

[25]''I have spoken of these matters very guardedly, but the time will come when this will not be necessary and I will tell you plainly all about the Father. [26]Then you will present your petitions over my signature![e] And I won't need to ask the Father to grant you these requests, [27]for the Father himself loves you dearly because you love me and believe that I came from the Father. [28]Yes, I came from the Father into the world and will leave the

---

d. Implied.   e. Literally, ''you shall ask *in my name.*'' The above paraphrase is the modern equivalent of this idea, otherwise obscure.

world and return to the Father.''

²⁹"At last you are speaking plainly,'' his disciples said, ''and not in riddles. ³⁰Now we understand that you know everything and don't need anyone to tell you anything.ᶠ From this we believe that you came from God.''

³¹"Do you finally believe this?'' Jesus asked. ³²"But the time is coming—in fact, it is here—when you will be scattered, each one returning to his own home, leaving me alone. Yet I will not be alone, for the Father is with me. ³³I have told you all this so that you will have peace of heart and mind. Here on earth you will have many trials and sorrows; but cheer up, for I have overcome the world.''

The Path to Eternal Life
Jn 17:1–8

¹When Jesus had finished saying all these things he looked up to heaven and said, ''Father, the time has come. Reveal the glory of your Son so that he can give the glory back to you. ²For you have given him authority over every man and woman in all the earth. He gives eternal life to each one you have given him. ³And this is the way to have eternal life—by knowing you, the only true God, and Jesus Christ, the one you sent to earth! ⁴I brought glory to you here on earth by doing everything you told me to. ⁵And now, Father, reveal my glory as I stand in your presence, the glory we shared before the world began.

⁶"I have told these men all about you. They were in the world, but then you gave them to me. Actually, they were always yours, and you gave them to me; and they have obeyed you. ⁷Now they know that everything I have is a gift from

f. Literally ''and need not that anyone should ask you,'' i.e., discuss what is true.

you, [8]for I have passed on to them the commands you gave me; and they accepted them and know of a certainty that I came down to earth from you, and they believe you sent me.''

Prayer for All Christians
Jn 17:9–26

[9]"My plea is not for the world but for those you have given me because they belong to you. [10]And all of them, since they are mine, belong to you; and you have given them back to me with everything else of yours, and so *they are my glory!* [11]Now I am leaving the world, and leaving them behind, and coming to you. Holy Father, keep them in your own care—all those you have given me—so that they will be united just as we are, with none missing. [12]During my time here I have kept safe within your family[a] all of these you gave me. I guarded them so that not one perished, except the son of hell, as the Scriptures foretold.

[13]"And now I am coming to you. I have told them many things while I was with them so that they would be filled with my joy. [14]I have given them your commands. And the world hates them because they don't fit in with it, just as I don't. [15]I'm not asking you to take them out of the world, but to keep them safe from Satan's power. [16]They are not part of this world any more than I am. [17]Make them pure and holy through teaching them your words of truth. [18]As you sent me into the world, I am sending them into the world, [19]and I consecrate myself to meet their need for growth in truth and holiness.

[20]"I am not praying for these alone but also for the future believers who will come to me because

---

a. Literally, "kept in your name those whom you have given me."

of the testimony of these. ²¹My prayer for all of them is that they will be of one heart and mind, just as you and I are, Father—that just as you are in me and I am in you, so they will be in us, and the world will believe you sent me.

²²"I have given them the glory you gave me—the glorious unity of being one, as we are—²³I in them and you in me, all being perfected into one—so that the world will know you sent me and will understand that you love them as much as you love me. ²⁴Father, I want them with me—these you've given me—so that they can see my glory. You gave me the glory because you loved me before the world began!

²⁵"O righteous Father, the world doesn't know you, but I do; and these disciples know you sent me. ²⁶And I have revealed you to them, and will keep on revealing you so that the mighty love you have for me may be in them, and I in them."

Jesus Leaves the Upper Room
Lk 22:39

³⁹Then, accompanied by the disciples, he left the upstairs room and went as usual to the Mount of Olives.

15.

THE PASSION AND DEATH OF JESUS

The Agony in the Garden
Jn 18:1–2, Mt 26:36–44, Lk 22:43–44, Mt 26:45–46

¹After saying these things Jesus crossed the Kidron ravine with his disciples and entered a grove of olive trees. ²Judas, the betrayer, knew this place, for Jesus had gone there many times with his disciples.

³⁶Then Jesus brought them to a garden grove, Gethsemane, and told them to sit down and wait while he went on ahead to pray. ³⁷He took Peter with him and Zebedee's two sons James and John, and began to be filled with anguish and despair.

> Gethsemane is an Aramaic word meaning "oil press."

³⁸Then he told them, "My soul is crushed with horror and sadness to the point of death...stay here...stay awake with me."

³⁹He went forward a little, and fell face downward on the ground, and prayed, "My Father! If it is possible, let this cup be taken away from me. But I want your will, not mine."

⁴⁰Then he returned to the three disciples and found them asleep. "Peter," he called, "couldn't you even stay awake with me one hour? ⁴¹Keep alert and pray. Otherwise temptation will overpower you. For the spirit indeed is willing, but

how weak the body is!''

⁴²Again he left them and prayed, ''My Father! If this cup cannot go away until I drink it all, your will be done.''

⁴³He returned to them again and found them sleeping, for their eyes were heavy, ⁴⁴so he went back to prayer the third time, saying the same things again. ⁴³Then an angel from heaven appeared and strengthened him, ⁴⁴for he was in such agony of spirit that he broke into a sweat of blood, with great drops falling to the ground as he prayed more and more earnestly.

⁴⁵Then he came to the disciples and said, ''Sleep on now and take your rest...but no! The time has come! I[e] am betrayed into the hands of evil men! ⁴⁶Up! Let's be going! Look! Here comes the man who is betraying me!''

The militia which came after Jesus probably left the city through the Casement Wall Gate. As it made its way north along the Kidron Valley, it could be seen by those on Mount Olivet, particularly since the soldiers carried torches.

The Betrayal
Jn 18:3, Mt 26:48–49, Lk 22:48, Jn 18:4–10,
Mt 26:52–56, Mk 14:51–52

³The chief priests and Pharisees had given Judas a squad of soldiers and police to accompany him. Now with blazing torches, lanterns, and weapons they arrived at the olive grove. ⁴⁸Judas had told them to arrest the man he greeted, for that would be the one they were after. ⁴⁹So now Judas came straight to Jesus and said, ''Hello, Master!'' and embraced[f] him in friendly fashion.

⁴⁸But Jesus said, ''Judas, how can you do this—betray the Messiah with a kiss?''

⁴,⁵Jesus finally realized all that was going to happen to him. Stepping forward to meet them he asked, ''Whom are you looking for?''

''Jesus of Nazareth,'' they replied.

---

e. Literally, ''the Son of Man.''   f. Literally, ''kissed,'' the greeting still used among men in Eastern lands.

"I am he, Jesus said. [6]And as he said it, they all fell backwards to the ground!

[7]Once more he asked them, "Whom are you searching for?"

And again they replied, "Jesus of Nazareth."

[8]"I told you I am he," Jesus said; "and since I am the one you are after, let these others go." [9]He did this to carry out the prophecy he had just made, "I have not lost a single one of those you gave me...."

[10]Then Simon Peter drew a sword and slashed off the right ear of Malchus, the High Priest's servant.

[52]"Put away your sword," Jesus told him. "Those using swords will get killed. [53]Don't you realize that I could ask my Father for thousands of angels to protect us, and he would send them instantly? [54]But if I did, how would the Scriptures be fulfilled that describe what is happening now?" [55]Then Jesus spoke to the crowd. "Am I some dangerous criminal," he asked, "that you had to arm yourselves with swords and clubs before you could arrest me? I was with you teaching daily in the Temple and you didn't stop me then. [56]But this is all happening to fulfill the words of the prophets as recorded in the Scriptures."

At that point, all the disciples deserted him and fled.

[51,52]There was, however, a young man following along behind, clothed only in a linen nightshirt.[h] When the mob tried to grab him, he escaped, though his clothes were torn off in the process, so that he ran away completely naked.

Some writers speculate that the young man was John Mark the Evangelist. This possibility gains weight if Jesus used the Mount Zion home of Mark's mother for the Passover Supper. At any rate, only Mark recounts this incident.

Jesus Is Taken to Annas
Jn 18:12–15, 18–24

[12]So the Jewish police, with the soldiers and their

---

h. Implied. Literally, "wearing only a linen cloth."

lieutenant, arrested Jesus and tied him. ¹³First they took him to Annas, the father-in-law of Caiaphas, the High Priest that year. ¹⁴Caiaphas was the one who told the other Jewish leaders, "Better that one should die for all." ¹⁵Simon Peter followed along behind, as did another of the disciples who was acquainted with the High Priest.

¹⁸The police and the household servants were standing around a fire they had made, for it was cold. And Peter stood there with them, warming himself.

¹⁹Inside, the High Priest began asking Jesus about his followers and what he had been teaching them.

²⁰Jesus replied, "What I teach is widely known, for I have preached regularly in the synagogue and Temple; I have been heard by all the Jewish leaders and teach nothing in private that I have not said in public. ²¹Why are you asking me this question? Ask those who heard me. You have some of them here. They know what I said."

²²One of the soldiers, standing there struck Jesus with his fist. "Is that the way to answer the High Priest?" he demanded.

²³"If I lied, prove it," Jesus replied. "Should you hit a man for telling the truth?"

²⁴Then Annas sent Jesus, bound, to Caiaphas the High Priest.

Annas had been deposed as high priest by the Romans in A.D. 15. However, in the Jewish mind the office was for life. He had been succeeded by his sons and son-in-law, so still had control. This is shown by the fact that Jesus was taken first to Annas.

Jesus Before the Supreme Court
Mt 26:57–68

⁵⁷Then the mob led him to the home of Caiaphas the High Priest, where all the Jewish leaders were gathering. ⁵⁸Meanwhile, Peter was following far to the rear, and came to the courtyard of the High Priest's house and went in and sat with the sol-

diers, and waited to see what was going to be done to Jesus.

⁵⁹The chief priests and, in fact, the entire Jewish Supreme Court assembled there and looked for witnesses who would lie about Jesus, in order to build a case against him that would result in a death sentence. ⁶⁰,⁶¹But even though they found many who agreed to be false witnesses, these always contradicted each other.

Finally two men were found who declared, "This man said, 'I am able to destroy the Temple of god and rebuild it in three days.'"

⁶²Then the High Priest stood up and said to Jesus, "Well, what about it? Did you say that, or didn't you?" ⁶³But Jesus remained silent.

Then the High Priest said to him, "I demand in the name of the living God that you tell us whether you claim to be the Messiah, the Son of God."

⁶⁴"Yes," Jesus said, "I am. And in the future you will see me, the Messiah,ᵉ sitting at the right hand of God and returning on the clouds of heaven."

⁶⁵,⁶⁶Then the High Priest tore at his own clothing, shouting, "Blasphemy! What need have we for other witnesses? You have all heard him say it! What is your verdict?"

They shouted, "Death!—Death!—Death!"

⁶⁷Then they spat in his face and struck him and some slapped him, ⁶⁸saying, "Prophesy to us, you Messiah! Who struck you that time?"

This is the revelation of the Messianic secret. The title of Messiah had been given only by Peter (Mk 8:29). The title of Son of God had been given only by evil spirits.

Peter Denies Jesus
Mt 26:69–72, Jn 18:26, Mt 26:74–75

⁶⁹Meanwhile, as Peter was sitting in the courtyard a girl came over and said to him, "You were with

---

e. Literally, "the Son of Man."

Jesus, for both of you are from Galilee.''g

70But Peter denied it loudly. ''I don't even know what you are talking about,'' he angrily declared.

71Later, out by the gate, another girl noticed him and said to those standing around, ''This man was with Jesus—from Nazareth.''

72Again Peter denied it, this time with an oath. ''I don't even know the man,'' he said.

But one of the household slaves of the High Priest—a relative of the man whose ear Peter had cut off—asked, ''Didn't I see you out there in the olive grove with Jesus?''

74Peter began to curse and swear. ''I don't even know the man,'' he said.

And immediately the cock crowed. 75Then Peter remembered what Jesus had said, ''Before the cock crows, you will deny me three times.''And he went away, crying bitterly.

Jesus is Taken to Pilate
Mt 27:1–2

1When it was morning, the chief priests and Jewish leaders met again to discuss how to induce the Roman government to sentence Jesus to death.a 2Then they sent him in chains to Pilate, the Roman governor.

The Sanhedrin did not have the power to pass a capital sentence. This had to be done by the Romans. Hence the task was to persuade Pilate, the Roman procurator, to give the judgment.

Judas Hangs Himself
Mt 27:3–10

3About that time Judas, who betrayed him, when he saw that Jesus had been condemned to die, changed his mind and deeply regretted what he had done,b and brought back the money to the

g. Literally, ''with Jesus the Galilean.''

a. Literally, ''took counsel against Jesus to put him to death.'' They did not have the authority themselves.

b. Literally, ''repented himself.''

chief priests and other Jewish leaders.

⁴"I have sinned," he declared, "for I have betrayed an innocent man."

"That's your problem," they retorted.

⁵Then he threw the money onto the floor of the Temple and went out and hanged himself. ⁶The chief priests picked the money up. "We can't put it in the collection," they said, "since it's against our laws to accept money paid for murder."

⁷They talked it over and finally decided to buy a certain field where the clay was used by potters, and to make it into a cemetery for foreigners who died in Jerusalem. ⁸That is why the cemetery is still called "The Field of Blood."

⁹This fulfilled the prophecy of Jeremiah which says, "They took the thirty pieces of silver—the price at which he was valued by the people of Israel—¹⁰and purchased a field from the potters as the Lord directed me."

Pilate Hears the Charges
Lk 23:1-2, Jn 18:28-32, Mk 15:3-5,
Jn 18:33-37, Lk 23:3-7

¹Then the entire Council took Jesus over to Pilate, the governor.[a] ²They began at once accusing him: "This fellow has been leading our people to ruin by telling them not to pay their taxes to the Roman government and by claiming he is our Messiah—a King."

²⁸His accusers wouldn't go in themselves for that would "defile"[a] them, they said, and they wouldn't be allowed to eat the Passover lamb. ²⁹So Pilate, the governor, went out to them and asked, "What is your charge against this man? What are you accusing him of doing?"

a. Implied.

a. By Jewish law, entering the house of a Gentile was a serious offense.

30"We wouldn't have arrested him if he weren't a criminal!" they retorted.

31"Then take him away and judge him yourselves by your own laws," Pilate told them.

"But we want him crucified," they demanded, "and your approval is required."b 32This fulfilled Jesus' prediction concerning the method of his execution.c

3,4Then the chief priests accused him of many crimes, and Pilate asked him, "Why don't you say something? What about all these charges against you?"

5But Jesus said no more, much to Pilate's amazement.

33Then Pilate went back into the palace and called for Jesus to be brought to him. "Are you the King of the Jews?" he asked him.

34"'King' as *you* use the word or as the *Jews* use it?" Jesus asked.d

35"Am I a Jew?" Pilate retorted. "Your own people and their chief priests brought you here. Why? What have you done?"

36Then Jesus answered, "I am not an earthly king. If I were, my followers would have fought when I was arrested by the Jewish leaders. But my Kingdom is not of the world."

37Pilate replied, "But you are a king then?"

"Yes," Jesus said."I was born for that purpose. And I came to bring truth to the world. All who love the truth are my followers."

3So Pilate asked him, "Are you their Messiah— their King?"b

"Yes," Jesus replied,"it is as you say."

4Then Pilate turned to the chief priests and to the mob and said, "So? That isn't a crime!"

b. Literally, "It is not lawful for us to put any man to death." c. This prophecy is recorded in Mt 20:19, which indicates his death by crucifixion, a practice under Roman law. d. A paraphrase of this verse—that goes beyond the limits of this book's paraphrasing—would be, "Do you mean their King, or their Messiah?" If Pilate was asking as the Roman governor, he would be inquiring whether Jesus was setting up a rebel government. But the Jews were using the word "King" to mean their religious ruler, the Messiah. Literally, this verse reads, "Are you saying this of yourself, or did someone else say it about me?"

b. Literally, "Are you the King of the Jews?"

⁵Then they became desperate. "But he is causing riots against the government everywhere he goes, all over Judea, from Galilee to Jerusalem!"

⁶"Is he then a Galilean?" Pilate asked.

⁷When they told him yes, Pilate said to take him to King Herod, for Galilee was under Herod's jurisdiction; and Herod happened to be in Jerusalem at the time.

The Romans had appointed Herod Antipas as tetrarch of Galilee and Peraea. He had no authority in Judea but Pilate was trying to pass the buck. Herod was probably in Jerusalem for the Passover holiday.

Herod Mocks Jesus
Lk 23:8–12

⁸Herod was delighted at the opportunity to see Jesus, for he had heard a lot about him and had been hoping to see him perform a miracle.

⁹He asked Jesus question after question, but there was no reply. ¹⁰Meanwhile, the chief priests and the other religious leaders stood there shouting their accusations.

¹¹Now Herod and his soldiers began mocking and ridiculing Jesus; and putting a kingly robe on him, they sent him back to Pilate. ¹²That day Herod and Pilate—enemies before—became fast friends.

Jesus is Scourged and Crowned with Thorns
Lk 23:13–16, Jn 19:1–3

¹³Then Pilate called together the chief priests and other Jewish leaders, along with the people, ¹⁴and announced his verdict:

"You brought this man to me, accusing him of leading a revolt against the Roman government.ᶜ I have examined him thoroughly on this point and find him innocent. ¹⁵Herod came to the same con-

c. Literally, "as one who perverts the people."

clusion and sent him back to us—nothing this man has done calls for the death penalty. ¹⁶I will therefore have him scourged with leaded thongs, and release him."

¹Then Pilate laid open Jesus' back with a leaded whip, ²and the soldiers made a crown of thorns and placed it on his head and robed him in royal purple. ³"Hail, 'King of the Jews!'" they mocked, and struck him with their fists.

"Behold the Man"
Jn 19:4–15

⁴Pilate went outside again and said to the Jews, "I am going to bring him out to you now, but understand clearly that I find him *not guilty*."

⁵Then Jesus came out wearing the crown of thorns and the purple robe. And Pilate said, "Behold the man!"

⁶At sight of him the chief priests and Jewish officials began yelling, "Crucify! Crucify!"

"*You* crucify him," Pilate said. "I find him *not guilty*."

⁷They replied, "By our laws he ought to die because he called himself the Son of God."

⁸When Pilate heard this, he was more frightened than ever. ⁹He took Jesus back into the palace again and asked him, "Where are you from?" but Jesus gave no answer.

¹⁰"You won't talk to me?" Pilate demanded. "Don't you realize that I have the power to release you or to crucify you?"

¹¹Then Jesus said, "You would have no power at all over me unless it were given to you from above. So those ᵃ who brought me to you have the greater sin."

a. Literally, "he."

¹²Then Pilate tried to release him, but the Jewish leaders told him, ''If you release this man, you are no friend of Caesar's. Anyone who declares himself a king is a rebel against Caesar.''

¹³At these words Pilate brought Jesus out to them again and sat down at the judgment bench on the stone-paved platform.ᵇ ¹⁴It was now about noon on the day before Passover.

And Pilate said to the Jews, ''Here is your king!''

¹⁵''Away with him,'' they yelled. ''Away with him—crucify him!''

''What? Crucify your king?'' Pilate asked.

''We have no king but Caesar,'' the chief priests shouted back.

Pilate Condemns Jesus to Die
Mt 27:15–25, Lk 23:24–25

¹⁵Now the governor's custom was to release one Jewish prisoner each year during the Passover celebration—anyone they wanted. ¹⁶This year there was a particularly notorious criminal in jail named Barabbas, ¹⁷and as the crowds gathered before Pilate's house that morning he asked them, ''Which shall I release to you—Barabbas, or Jesus your Messiah?''ᵈ ¹⁸For he knew very well that the Jewish leaders had arrested Jesus out of envy because of his popularity with the people.

¹⁹Just then, as he was presiding over the court, Pilate's wife sent him this message: ''Leave that good man alone; for I had a terrible nightmare concerning him last night.''

²⁰Meanwhile the chief priests and Jewish officials persuaded the crowds to ask for Barabbas' release, and for Jesus' death. ²¹So when the gover-

Some biblical commentators picture Barabbas as one who engaged in guerrilla war against the Romans because of other amnesties elsewhere. However, Scripture gives no indication of this.

b. Literally, ''the judgment seat in a place that is called The Pavement, but in Hebrew, Gabbatha.''

d. Literally, ''Jesus who is called Christ.''

nor asked again,[e] "Which of these two shall I release to you?" the crowd shouted back their reply: "Barabbas!"

²²"Then what shall I do with Jesus, your Messiah?" Pilate asked.

And they shouted, "Crucify him!"

²³"Why?" Pilate demanded. "What has he done wrong?" But they kept shouting, "Crucify! Crucify!"

²⁴When Pilate saw that he wasn't getting anywhere, and that a riot was developing, he sent for a bowl of water and washed his hands before the crowd, saying, "I am innocent of the blood of this good man. The responsibility is yours!"

²⁵And the mob yelled back, "His blood be on us and on our children!"

²⁴So Pilate sentenced Jesus to die as they demanded. ²⁵And he released Barabbas, the man in prison for insurrection and murder, at their request. But he delivered Jesus over to them to do with as they would.

The Way of the Cross
Jn 19:17, Mt 27:31–32, Mk 15:21, Lk 23:27–32

¹⁷So they had him at last.

³¹After the mockery, they took off the robe and put his own garment on him again, and took him out to crucify him. ³²As they were on the way to the execution grounds they came across a man from Cyrene, in Africa—Simon was his name—and forced him to carry Jesus' cross. (Simon is the father of Alexander and Rufus.) ²⁷Great crowds trailed along behind, and many grief-stricken women.

Since Simon's sons are mentioned by name, they were probably Christians well-known in the early Church. Cyrene was a city in North Africa (modern Libya) that had a large Jewish population. Since he was coming in from the fields (Mk 15:21), he was probably a farmer, resident of Jerusalem.

e. Implied.

²⁸But Jesus turned and said to them, "Daughters of Jerusalem, don't weep for me, but for yourselves and for your children. ²⁹For the days are coming when the women who have no children will be counted fortunate indeed. ³⁰Mankind will beg the mountains to fall on them and crush them, and the hills to bury them. ³¹For if such things as this are done to me, the Living Tree, what will they do to you?"ᵉ

The Crucifixion
Mk 15:22–23, Lk 23:34, Mk 15:25, 27–28, Jn 19:19–22

²²And they brought Jesus to a place called Golgotha. (Golgotha means skull.) ²³Wine drugged with bitter herbs was offered to him there, but he refused it.

³⁴"Father, forgive these people," Jesus said, "for they don't know what they are doing."

²⁵It was about nine o'clock in the morning when the crucifixion took place.

²⁷Two robbers were also crucified that morning, their crosses on either side of his. ²⁸ᵇAnd so the Scripture was fulfilled that said, "He was counted among evil men." ¹⁹And Pilate posted a sign over him reading, "Jesus of Nazareth, the King of the Jews." ²⁰The place where Jesus was crucified was near the city; and the signboard was written in Hebrew, Latin, and Greek, so that many people read it.

²¹Then the chief priests said to Pilate, "Change it from 'The King of the Jews' to '*He said,* I am King of the Jews.'"

²²Pilate replied, "What I have written, I have written. It stays exactly as it is."

Solid tradition places Golgotha as a rocky knoll just northwest of the city gate of the road to Joppa. The Romans crucified along roads as an example to those passing by.

The Scripture is Is 53:12.

---

e. Literally, "For if they do this when the tree is green, what will happen when it is dry?"

b. Verse 28 is omitted in some of the ancient manuscripts. The quotation is from Is 53:12.

The Soldiers Cast Lots
Jn 19:23–25

23,24When the soldiers had crucified Jesus, they put his garments into four piles, one for each of them. But they said, "Let's not tear up his robe," for it was seamless. "Let's throw dice to see who gets it." This fulfilled the Scripture that says, "They divided my clothes among them, and cast lots for my robe."c 25So that is what they did.

The Crowds Mock Jesus
Mt 27:39–43

39And the people passing by hurled abuse, shaking their heads at him and saying, 40"So! You can destroy the Temple and build it again in three days, can you? Well, then, come on down from the cross if you are the Son of God!"

41,42,43And the chief priests and Jewish leaders also mocked him. "He saved others," they scoffed, "but he can't save himself! So you are the King of Israel, are you? Come down from the cross and we'll believe you! He trusted God—let God show his approval by delivering him! Didn't he say, 'I am God's Son'?"

The Good Thief
Lk 23:39–43

39One of the criminals hanging beside him scoffed, "So you're the Messiah, are you? Prove it by saving yourself—and us, too, while you're at it!"

40,41But the other criminal protested. "Don't you even fear God when you are dying? We deserve to

c. Ps 22:18.

die for our evil deeds, but this man hasn't done one thing wrong.'' ⁴²Then he said, ''Jesus, remember me when you come into your Kingdom.''

⁴³And Jesus replied, ''Today you will be with me in Paradise. This is a solemn promise.''

Jesus Entrusts His Mother to John
Jn 19:25–27

²⁵Standing near the cross were Jesus' mother, Mary, his aunt, the wife of Cleopas, and Mary Magdalene. ²⁶When Jesus saw his mother standing there beside me, his close friend,ᵈ he said to her, ''He is your son.''

²⁷And to meᵉ he said, ''She is your mother!'' And from then on I took her into my home.

It is not clear whether John means three or four women.

Jesus Dies
Mt 27:45–47, Jn 19:28–30, Lk 23:46–47, Mt 27:51–56

⁴⁵That afternoon, the whole earthᶠ was covered with darkness for three hours, from noon until three o'clock.

⁴⁶About three o'clock, Jesus shouted, ''Eli, Eli, lama sabachthani,'' which means, ''My God, my God, why have you forsaken me?''

⁴⁷Some of the bystanders misunderstood and thought he was calling for Elijah.

²⁸Jesus knew that everything was now finished, and to fulfill the Scriptures said, ''I'm thirsty.'' ²⁹A jar of sour wine was sitting there, so a sponge was soaked in it and put on a hyssop branch and held up to his lips.

Ps 69:22.

³⁰When Jesus had tastedᶠ it, he said, ''It is finished,'' and bowed his head and dismissed his spirit.

d. Literally, ''standing by the disciple whom he loved.''   e. Literally, ''to the disciple.''

f. Or, ''land.''

f. Literally, ''had received.''

⁴⁶Then Jesus shouted, "Father, I commit my spirit to you," and with those words he died.ʰ

⁴⁷When the captain of the Roman military unit handling the executions saw what had happened, he was stricken with awe before God and said, "Surely this man was innocent."ⁱ

⁵¹And look! The curtain secluding the Holiest Placeᵍ in the Temple was split apart from top to bottom; and the earth shook, and rocks broke, ⁵²and tombs opened, and many godly men and women who had died came back to life again. ⁵³After Jesus' resurrection, they left the cemetery and went into Jerusalem, and appeared to many people there.

⁵⁴The soldiers at the crucifixion and their sergeant were terribly frightened by the earthquake and all that happened. They exclaimed, "Surely this was God's Son."ʰ

⁵⁵And many women who had come down from Galilee with Jesus to care for him were watching from a distance. ⁵⁶Among them were Mary Magdalene and Mary the mother of James and Joseph, and the mother of James and John (the sons of Zebedee).

Jesus Is Pierced with a Lance
Jn 19:31–37

³¹The Jewish leaders didn't want the victims hanging there the next day, which was the Sabbath (and a very special Sabbath at that, for it was the Passover), so they asked Pilate to order the legs of the men broken to hasten death; then their bodies could be taken down. ³²So the soldiers came and broke the legs of the two men crucified with Jesus; ³³but when they came to him, they saw

h. Literally, "yielded up the spirit."   i. Literally, "righteous."
g. Implied.   h. Or, "a godly man."

that he was dead already, so they didn't break his. [34]However, one of the soldiers pierced his side with a spear, and blood and water flowed out. [35]I saw all this myself and have given an accurate report so that you also can believe.[g] [36,37]The soldiers did this in fulfillment of the Scripture that says, "Not one of his bones shall be broken," and, "They shall look on him whom they pierced."

See Ex 12:46, Ps 34:21, Zech 13:1.

Jesus Is Buried
Mk 15:42–45, Jn 19:38–42, Mk 23:55–56, Mk 15:47, Mt 27:62–66

[42,43]This all happened the day before the Sabbath. Late that afternoon Joseph from Arimathea, an honored member of the Jewish Supreme Court (who personally was eagerly expecting the arrival of God's kingdom), gathered his courage and went to Pilate and asked for Jesus' body.

[44]Pilate couldn't believe that Jesus was already dead so he called for the Roman officer in charge and asked him. [45]The officer confirmed the fact, and Pilate told Joseph he could have the body. [38]So he came and took it away. [39]Nicodemus, the man who had come to Jesus at night,[h] came too, bringing a hundred pounds of embalming ointment made from myrrh and aloes. [40]Together they wrapped Jesus' body in a long linen cloth saturated with the spices, as is the Jewish custom of burial. [41]The place of crucifixion was near a grove of trees,[i] where there was a new tomb, never used before. [42]And so, because of the need for haste before the Sabbath, and because the tomb was close at hand, they laid him there.

At last Nicodemus goes public with his belief.

[55]As the body was taken away, the women from Galilee followed and saw it carried into the tomb.

g. Literally, "And he who has seen has borne witness, and his witness is true; and he knows what he says is true, that you also may believe." h. See Chapter 3. i. Literally, "a garden."

[56]Then they went home and prepared spices and ointments to embalm him; but by the time they were finished it was the Sabbath, so they rested all that day as required by the Jewish law.

[47](Mary Magdalene and Mary the mother of Joses were watching as Jesus was laid away.)

[62]The next day—at the close of the first day of the Passover ceremonies[i]—the chief priests and Pharisees went to Pilate, [63]and told him, "Sir, that liar once said, 'After three days I will come back to life again.' [64]So we request an order from you sealing the tomb until the third day, to prevent his disciples from coming and stealing his body and then telling everyone he came back to life! If that happens we'll be worse off than we were at first."

[65]"Use your own Temple police," Pilate told them. "They can guard it safely enough."

[66]So they sealed[j] the stone and posted guards to protect it from intrusion.

i. Implied; literally, "on the morrow, which is after the Preparation."   j. This was done by stringing a cord across the rock, the cord being sealed at each end with clay.

16.

THE FINAL VICTORY

The Empty Tomb
Mk 16:1–8, Lk 24:8–11

¹The next evening, when the Sabbath ended, Mary Magdalene and Salome and Mary the mother of James went out and purchased embalming spices.

²Early the following morning, just at sunrise, they carried them out to the tomb. ³On the way they were discussing how they could ever roll aside the huge stone from the entrance.

⁴But when they arrived they looked up and saw that the stone—a *very* heavy one—was already moved away and the entrance was open! ⁵So they entered the tomb—and there on the right sat a young man clothed in white. The women were startled, ⁶but the angel said, "Don't be so surprised. Aren't you looking for Jesus, the Nazarene who was crucified? He isn't here! He has come back to life! Look, that's where his body was lying. ⁷Now go and give this message to his disciples including Peter:

'"Jesus is going ahead of you to Galilee. You will see him there, just as he told you before he died!"'

⁸The women fled from the tomb, trembling and

bewildered, too frightened to talk.

⁸Then they remembered, ⁹and rushed back to Jerusalemᵇ to tell his eleven disciples—and everyone else—what had happened. ¹⁰(The women who went to the tomb were Mary Magdalene and Joanna and Mary the mother of James, and several others.) ¹¹But the story sounded like a fairy tale to the men—they didn't believe it.

The Guards Are Bribed
Mt 28:11-15

¹¹As the women were on the way into the city, some of the Temple police who had been guarding the tomb went to the chief priests and told them what had happened. ¹²,¹³A meeting of all the Jewish leaders was called, and it was decided to bribe the police to say they had all been asleep when Jesus' disciples came during the night and stole his body.

¹⁴"If the governor hears about it," the Council promised, "we'll stand up for you and everything will be all right."

¹⁵So the police accepted the bribe and said what they were told to. Their story spread widely among the Jews, and is still believed by them to this very day.

John's Account of the Morning
Jn 20:1-18

¹Early Sundayᵃ morning, while it was still dark, Mary Magdalene came to the tomb and found that the stone was rolled aside from the entrance.

²She ran and found Simon Peter and meᵇ and said, "They have taken the Lord's body out of the

b. Literally, "returned from the tomb."

a. Literally, "on the first day of the week."   b. Literally, "the other disciple whom Jesus loved."

tomb, and I don't know where they have put him!''

3,4We[c] ran to the tomb to see; I[d] outran Peter and got there first, 5and stooped and looked in and saw the linen cloth lying there, but I didn't go in. 6Then Simon Peter arrived and went on inside. He also noticed the cloth lying there, 7while the swath that had covered Jesus' head was rolled up in a bundle and was lying at the side. 8Then I went in too, and saw, and believed [that he had risen[e]]— 9for until then we hadn't realized that the Scriptures said he would come to life again!

10We[f] went on home, 11and by that time Mary had returned to the tomb[e] and was standing outside crying. And as she wept, she stooped and looked in 12and saw two white-robed angels sitting at the head and foot of the place where the body of Jesus had been lying.

13''Why are you crying?'' the angels asked her.

''Because they have taken away my Lord,'' she replied, ''and I don't know where they have put him.''

14She glanced over her shoulder and saw someone standing behind her. It was Jesus, but she didn't recognize him!

15''Why are you crying?''he asked her. ''Whom are you looking for?''

She thought he was the gardener. ''Sir,'' she said, ''if you have taken him away, tell me where you have put him, and I will go and get him.''

16''Mary!''Jesus said. She turned toward him.

''Master!'' she exclaimed.

17''Don't touch me,'' he cautioned, ''for I haven't yet ascended to the Father. But go find my brothers and tell them that I ascend to my Father and your Father, my God and your God.''

18Mary Magdalene found the disciples and told

---

c. Literally, ''Peter and the other disciple.''   d. Literally, ''the other disciple also, who came first.''   .e. Implied.   f. Literally, ''the disciples.''

them, "I have seen the Lord!" Then she gave them his message.

Jesus Appears on the Road to Emmaus
Lk 24:13–34

¹³That same day, Sunday, two of Jesus' followers were walking to the village of Emmaus, seven miles out of Jerusalem. ¹⁴As they walked along they were talking of Jesus' death, ¹⁵when suddenly Jesus himself came along and joined them and began walking beside them. ¹⁶But they didn't recognize him, for God kept them from it.

¹⁷"You seem to be in a deep discussion about something," he said. "What are you so concerned about?" They stopped short, sadness written across their faces. ¹⁸And one of them, Cleopas, replied, "You must be the only person in Jerusalem who hasn't heard about the terrible things that happened there last week."[c]

¹⁹"What things?" Jesus asked.

"The things that happened to Jesus, the Man from Nazareth," they said. "He was a Prophet who did incredible miracles and was a mighty Teacher, highly regarded by both God and man. ²⁰But the chief priests and our religious leaders arrested him and handed him over to the Roman government to be condemned to death, and they crucified him. ²¹We had thought he was the glorious Messiah and that he had come to rescue Israel.

"And now, besides all this—which happened three days ago—²²,²³some women from our group of his followers were at his tomb early this morning and came back with an amazing report that his body was missing, and that they had seen some angels there who told them Jesus is alive! ²⁴Some

Is Cleopas of Jn 19:25 the same as Luke's? Probably. He is possibly Luke's source for this story.

c. Literally, "in these days."

of our men ran out to see, and sure enough, Jesus' body was gone, just as the women had said."

²⁵Then Jesus said to them, "You are such fool- ish, foolish people! You find it so hard to believe all that the prophets wrote in the Scriptures! ²⁶Wasn't it clearly predicted by the prophets that the Messiah would have to suffer all these things before entering his time of glory?"

²⁷Then Jesus quoted them passage after passage from the writings of the prophets, beginning with the book of Genesis and going right on through the Scriptures, explaining what the passages meant and what they said about himself.

²⁸By this time they were nearing Emmaus and the end of their journey. Jesus would have gone on, ²⁹but they begged him to stay the night with them, as it was getting late. So he went home with them. ³⁰As they sat down to eat, he asked God's blessing on the food and then took a small loaf of bread and broke it and was passing it over to them, ³¹when suddenly—it was as though their eyes were opened—they recognized him! And at that moment he disappeared!

³²They began telling each other how their hearts had felt strangely warm as he talked with them and explained the Scriptures during the walk down the road. ³³,³⁴Within the hour they were on their way back to Jerusalem, where the eleven dis- ciples and the other followers of Jesus greeted them with these words, "The Lord has really risen! He appeared to Peter!"

Jesus Appears to the Disciples
Lk 24:35–37, Jn 20:19–23, Lk 24:38–43

³⁵Then the two from Emmaus told their story of

how Jesus had appeared to them as they were walking along the road and how they had recognized him as he was breaking the bread. ³⁶And just as they were telling about it, Jesus himself was suddenly standing there among them, and greeted them. ³⁷But the whole group was terribly frightened, thinking they were seeing a ghost! ¹⁹After greeting them, ²⁰he showed them his hands and side. And how wonderful was their joy as they saw their Lord!

²¹He spoke to them again and said, "As the Father has sent me, even so I am sending you." ²²Then he breathed on them and told them, "Receive the Holy Spirit. ²³If you forgive anyone's sins, they are forgiven. If you refuse to forgive them, they are unforgiven.

³⁸"Why are you frightened?" he asked. "Why do you doubt that it is really I? ³⁹Look at my hands! Look at my feet! You can see that it is I, myself! Touch me and make sure that I am not a ghost! For ghosts don't have bodies, as you see that I do!" ⁴⁰As he spoke, he held out his hands for them to see [the marks of the nails^d], and showed them [the wounds in^d] his feet.

⁴¹Still they stood there undecided, filled with joy and doubt.

Then he asked them, "Do you have anything here to eat?"

⁴²They gave him a piece of broiled fish, ⁴³and he ate it as they watched!

Doubting Thomas
Jn 20:24–29

²⁴One of the disciples, Thomas, "The Twin," was not there at the time with the others. ²⁵When they

d. Implied.

kept telling him, "We have seen the Lord," he replied, "I won't believe it unless I see the nail wounds in his hands—and put my fingers into them—and place my hand into his side."

²⁶Eight days later the disciples were together again, and this time Thomas was with them. The doors were locked; but suddenly, as before, Jesus was standing among them and greeting them.

²⁷Then he said to Thomas, "Put your finger into my hands. Put your hand into my side. Don't be faithless any longer. Believe!"

²⁸"My Lord and my God!" Thomas said.

²⁹Then Jesus told him, "You believe because you have seen me. But blessed are those who haven't seen me and believe anyway."

The Great Command
Mt 28:16–20

¹⁶Then the eleven disciples left for Galilee, going to the mountain where Jesus had said they would find him. ¹⁷There they met him and worshiped him—but some of them weren't sure it really was Jesus!

¹⁸He told the disciples, "I have been given all authority in heaven and earth. ¹⁹Therefore go and make disciples in[b] all the nations, baptizing them into the name of the Father and of the Son and of the Holy Spirit, ²⁰and then teach these new disciples to obey all the commands I have given you; and be sure of this—that I am with you always, even to the end of the world."[c]

Peter Is Again Tested and Approved
Jn 21:1–23

¹Later Jesus appeared again to the disciples beside

b. Literally, "of."
c. Or, "age."

the Lake of Galilee. This is how it happened:

²A group of us were there—Simon Peter, Thomas, "The Twin," Nathanael from Cana in Galilee, my brother James and I[a] and two other disciples.

³Simon Peter said, "I'm going fishing."

"We'll come too," we all said. We did, but caught nothing all night. ⁴At dawn we saw a man standing on the beach but couldn't see who he was.

⁵He called, "Any fish, boys?"[b]

"No," we replied.

⁶Then he said, "Throw out your net on the right-hand side of the boat, and you'll get plenty of them!" So we did, and couldn't draw in the net because of the weight of the fish, there were so many!

⁷Then I[c] said to Peter, "It is the Lord!" At that, Simon Peter put on his tunic (for he was stripped to the waist) and jumped into the water [and swam ashore[d]]. ⁸The rest of us stayed in the boat and pulled the loaded net to the beach, about 300 feet away. ⁹When we got there, we saw that a fire was kindled and fish were frying over it, and there was bread.

¹⁰"Bring some of the fish you've just caught," Jesus said. ¹¹So Simon Peter went out and dragged the net ashore. By his count there were 153 large fish; and yet the net hadn't torn.

¹²"Now come and have some breakfast!" Jesus said; and none of us dared ask him if he really was the Lord, for we were quite sure of it. ¹³Then Jesus went around serving us the bread and fish.

¹⁴This was the third time Jesus had appeared to us since his return from the dead.

¹⁵After breakfast Jesus said to Simon Peter, "Simon, son of John, do you love me more than

a. Literally, "the sons of Zebedee." b. Literally, "children." c. Literally, "that disciple therefore whom Jesus loved." d. Implied.

these others?''ᵉ

"Yes," Peter replied, "You know I am your friend."

"Then feed my lambs," Jesus told him.

¹⁶Jesus repeated the question: "Simon, son of John, do you *really* love me?"

"Yes, Lord," Peter said, "you know I am your friend."

"Then take care of my sheep," Jesus said.

¹⁷Once more he asked him, "Simon, son of John, are you even my friend?"

Peter was grieved at the way Jesus asked the question this third time. "Lord, you know my heart;ᶠ you know I am," he said.

Jesus said, "Then feed my little sheep. ¹⁸When you were young, you were able to do as you liked and go wherever you wanted to; but when you are old, you will stretch out your hands and others will direct you and take you where you don't want to go." ¹⁹Jesus said this to let him know what kind of death he would die to glorify God. Then Jesus told him, "Follow me."

²⁰Peter turned around and saw the disciple Jesus loved following, the one who had leaned around at supper that time to ask Jesus, "Master, which of us will betray you?" ²¹Peter asked Jesus, "What about him, Lord? What sort of death will he die?''ᵍ

²²Jesus replied, "If I want him to liveʰ until I return, what is that to you? *You* follow me."

²³So the rumor spread among the brotherhood that that disciple wouldn't die! But that isn't what Jesus said at all! He only said, "If I want him to liveʰ until I come, what is that to you?"

---

e. Literally, "more than these."See Mk 14:29.   f. Literally, "all things."   g. Implied. Literally, "and this man, what?"   h. Literally, "tarry."

Other Appearances
Acts 1:3–5, Lk 24:44–49, Acts 1:6–8

³During the forty days after his crucifixion he appeared to the apostles from time to time, actually alive, and proved to them in many ways that it was really he himself they were seeing. And on these occasions he talked to them about the Kingdom of God.

⁴In one of these meetings he told them not to leave Jerusalem until the Holy Spirit came upon them in fulfillment of the Father's promise, a matter he had previously discussed with them.

⁵"John baptized you with^b water," he reminded them, "but you shall be baptized with^b the Holy Spirit in just a few days."

⁴⁴Then he said, "When I was with you before, don't you remember my telling you that everything written about me by Moses and the prophets and in the Psalms must all come true?" ⁴⁵Then he opened their minds to understand at last these many Scriptures! ⁴⁶And he said, "Yes, it was written long ago that the Messiah must suffer and die and rise again from the dead on the third day; ⁴⁷and that this message of salvation should be taken from Jerusalem to all the nations: *There is forgiveness of sins for all who turn to me.* ⁴⁸You have seen these prophecies come true.

⁴⁹"And now I will send the Holy Spirit^e upon you, just as my Father promised. Don't begin telling others^f yet—stay here in the city until the Holy Spirit comes and fills you with power from heaven."

⁶And another time when he appeared to them, they asked him, "Lord, are you going to free Israel [from Rome^c] now and restore us as an independent nation?"

b. Or, "in."

e. Implied. Literally, "the promise of my Father." f. Literally, "but wait here in the city until. . . ." The paraphrase relates this to verse 47.

c. Implied.

7"The Father sets those dates," he replied, "and they are not for you to know. 8But when the Holy Spirit has come upon you, you will receive power to testify about me with great effect, to the people in Jerusalem, throughout Judea, in Samaria, and to the ends of the earth, about my death and resurrection."

The Ascension
Lk 24:50, Acts 1:9–12, Lk 24:52–53

50Then Jesus led them out along the road[g] to Bethany, and lifting his hands to heaven, he blessed them.

9It was not long afterwards that he rose into the sky and disappeared into a cloud, leaving them staring after him. 10As they were straining their eyes for another glimpse, suddenly two white-robed men were standing there among them, 11and said, "Men of Galilee, why are you standing here staring at the sky? Jesus has gone away to heaven, and some day, just as he went, he will return!"

12They were at the Mount of Olives when this happened, so now they walked the half mile back to Jerusalem filled with mighty joy, 52and were continually in the Temple, praising God.

Conclusion
Jn 20:30–31, 21:25

30,31Jesus' disciples saw him do many other miracles besides the ones told about in this book, but these are recorded so that you will believe that he is the Messiah, the Son of God, and that believ-

g. Implied. Bethany was a mile or so away, across the valley on the Mount of Olives.

ing in him you will have life.

[25]And I suppose that if all the other events in Jesus' life were written, the whole world could hardly contain the books!